to

Think Korean

The InterAct Series

Learning to Think Korean

A Guide to Living and Working in Korea

L. Robert Kohls

First published by Intercultural Press. For information contact:

Intercultural Press
PO Box 700
Yarmouth, ME 04096 USA
001-207-846-5168
Fax: 001-207-846-5181
www.interculturalpress.com

Nicholas Brealey Publishing
36 John Street
London, WC1N 2AT, UK
44-207-430-0224
Fax: 44-207-404-8311
www.nbrealey-books.com

Production and cover design by Patty J. Topel

Printed in the United States of America

05   04   03   02   01   1   2   3   4   5

Library of Congress Cataloging-in-Publication Data

Kohls, L. Robert.
Learning to think Korean: a guide to living and working in Korea / L. Robert Kohls.
   p.   cm.—(The InterAct Series)
Includes bibliographical references.
ISBN 1-877864-87-0
1. Korea (South)   2. National characteristics, Korean.
I. Title.   II. Series.

DS902.K516   2001
306'.095195—dc21   2001039213

Dedication

This book is dedicated to
the people of Korea
who taught me not only
all I know about Korea,
but also much about
my own country, America,
and about Life,
and about who I am.

Table of Contents

Foreword: My Love Affair with Korea

Not too long ago, I celebrated the fiftieth anniversary of my love affair with Korea. Long before most Americans* had even heard of Korea, it was *in my blood* and a regular part of my daily thoughts.

When I graduated from high school, I was fortunate enough to have had an uncle who decided that the best gift he could give me, before I went off to university, was to let me have a profound personal experience with Asia, so he sent me off to spend a couple of years in Japan and Korea at his expense.

I have not been the same since. That experience literally changed my life, and although I could not know it at the time, it set the course of my future and prepared me for a profession that did not even exist at the time—preparing

---

* Although I am well aware that the United States is only one of the many countries that share the two continents of the Americas, I have elected to follow the convention of referring to the citizens of the United States as "Americans." I have decided to do this because it is such a well-established convention and because we do not have a simple, satisfactory alternative. I humbly ask the citizens of Canada, Mexico, and all of the Central and South American countries to allow me to refer simply to Americans in this book.

people who were born and raised in one country to live and work effectively in other countries.

My uncle was your uncle, too—Uncle Sam—and the time was the end of the Second World War. I was one of the U.S. Army troops who liberated Korea from its Japanese occupation period (1910–1945). That much is certain. But what I cannot comprehend or explain is why, among all the hundreds of G.I.s I knew who had the same experience, I was the only one who fell hopelessly in love with Korea.[†] Why was I the only one who found Korean culture fascinating and rich and even *familiar*, although it was so completely different from my own? Why was I the one who would be pulled back to Korea again and again for the rest of my life?

After my Korean experience, I returned to the States to finish my undergraduate degree, to marry Norma, and to begin teaching in a small community college in northern Iowa, all the time with an eye to figuring out how to return to Korea. When the Korean War (1950–1953) broke out, my mission changed slightly; I began to focus on finding ways for Norma and me to return to Korea as soon as the war ended, to assist in repairing the devastation taking place. I was fortunately able to infect Norma with my contagious love for Korea, so she was as eager to go help as I, in whatever way we could, with Korea's reconstruction; she was to become the first foreign civilian woman to be allowed into the country in 1953.

In the small Iowa town where I was teaching, the principal of one of the elementary schools happened to be a Mennonite who had served as a relief worker with the Mennonite Central Committee (MCC) in China between 1945 and the communist takeover in 1949. Aware of my desire to return to

---

[†] Although I was the only one I knew in the 24th Corps who seemed to be favorably impressed with Korea from 1945 to 1950, indeed, several others eventually became Korea experts.

Korea, he urged us to consider serving with MCC. After the end of the Korean War, MCC accepted us as relief workers—our assignment, to establish and build (from the ground up) a vocational school, middle school, and high school for boys orphaned by the war.

As a result, Norma and I are the "parents" of two hundred Korean sons, now in their fifties and sixties, spread over South Korea, all still useful and contributing citizens of the country. The three years (1953–1956) that we were headmaster and headmistress of the Mennonite Vocational School for Older Orphan Boys in Kyong San, Korea, were among the most difficult, but also the richest and happiest years of our lives, and nothing describes them better than the Peace Corps motto, "The toughest job you'll ever love." We have also described these three years as "our Pre-Peace Corps Peace Corps assignment." The MCC was one of the private voluntary organizations whose relief programs served as a model for the newly formed Peace Corps in 1961.

Our next call to return to Korea came in 1963, just as I was finishing my Ph.D. thesis. Our good fried, the director of the Korea office of Christian Children's Fund (CCF) in Seoul, asked me to serve as acting director of CCF during his year's furlough at CCF headquarters. We quickly accepted and spent 1963 and 1964 in Korea. CCF is one of several similar organizations that manage the contributions of thousands of sponsors who send monthly contributions to support children in dozens of countries around the world. At that time CCF supported one hundred orphanages all over South Korea. During this period we adopted our Korean-American daughter, Kathy.

My next contact with Korea was as a trainer for Peace Corps in 1967. Through a series of contacts and some fortuitous good luck, I was hired by Westinghouse, the first of a number of major private companies to be granted contracts by the Peace Corps, to design and conduct a training program for the Peace Corps. It was at this time that the new field of training was being reshaped. The then-ubiquitous on-the-job training (still very similar to the apprenticeship learning of the Middle Ages) was miraculously being transformed into the experiential learning we know as training today. At that time the Peace Corps was one of the most exciting clients of this new cross-cultural training. They were then sufficiently funded to allow a favorable ratio of trainers (and returned Peace Corps volunteers) to trainees, and they were willing to trust the trainers to experiment in inventing new ways to orient the young volunteers to the reality of living and working in Third-World‡ and non-Western countries they had little if any knowledge of.

My initial venture into Peace Corps training, then, gave me my first experience as a cross-cultural trainer. The ultimate effect of this experience was to make it extremely difficult for me to return to the university classroom, where class size and the physical limitations of the teaching environment made it impossible to employ the dynamic experiential methods I had been introduced to in the Peace Corps training programs. Consequently, I had enormous reentry problems returning to the university classroom.

---

‡ I am, of course, aware of the trend to refer to what we once called the Third World as "Newly Industrialized Countries" or "Emerging Economies," but these designators do not cover the countries that are still not developing, industrially or economically, and that show no indication of wanting to do so. The term *Third World* is not meant to imply that the countries so designated are not first or second in terms of importance in anyone's estimation. It still describes countries (about 120 or 130 of them at last count) that have made a conscious decision to follow their own way, a third way—neither the capitalist nor the communist political philosophies (as it was first intended) nor the Western or Asian philosophical approaches to the interpretation of reality. I am therefore forced to use it until we are able to create a more acceptable label.

Even so, when Westinghouse phoned me to get my agreement to direct two more Peace Corps-Korea training programs the following summer (overlapping again into the fall
semester), I had no alternative but to turn them down. I
could not, after all, expect the university to give me a leave
of absence every other semester forever or to impose the
burden upon myself of re-experiencing such difficulties in
returning to the classroom over and over. Westinghouse
wasn't finished with me, though, and kept pursuing me to do
more Peace Corps training until, finally, they offered me a
full-time position at twice my university salary.

In brief, this is how Korea and my experiences there were
responsible for converting me from university professor to
cross-cultural trainer, and now author of this book, which is
aimed at helping other Americans learn to think Korean.

Norma and I plan, if we can squeeze it in before this
lifetime ends, to spend two more years in Korea, two more in
China, and two more in Japan. While we have experience
living in all three East Asian countries, we want to be able to
sort out more systematically and at greater depth than we
have been able thus far the specific similarities and differences among these three Confucian-based cultures that are so
dear to us.

I want to close this personal account of the past half
century of my life by sharing a secret with my readers. I must
ask you to keep this in absolute confidence, however, because
evidence of bias circulated about a cross-cultural trainer is
not good. In half a century of interacting with Asians from all
fifteen countries[§] on the Asian side of the Pacific Rim, Norma
and I have personally found Koreans to be among the warmest, most congenial people we have ever gotten to know. We
have also found it possible to have the most emotionally

[§] Australia, China, Hong Kong, Indonesia, Japan, Laos, Malaysia,
New Zealand, North Korea, Philippines, Singapore, South Korea, Taiwan, Thailand, and Vietnam.

rewarding relationships with Koreans of any people anywhere in the world.

So, we recommend Korea to you, without reservation, and we hope *Learning to Think Korean* will provide guidance on how most effectively to interact with Koreans and adapt to their culture. This book is designed to help you understand how Koreans *think*, to provide insights into value differences that affect behavior, and to offer specific recommendations on how to make your stay in Korea as rich and rewarding as possible.

Acknowledgments

I would like to express my indebtedness to the large number of individuals who made it possible for me to write this book. Foremost are the people of Korea, many of whom I know intimately and others with whom I have interacted for only a brief moment and whose names and life histories I have never known. The dedication which appears in the front of this book was written to be taken seriously in acknowledging the literally thousands of Koreans who have been my teachers—my *sŏnseng*—most of whom never knew how much they taught me or how deeply indebted to them I would be.

I cannot mention everyone, but I do want to identify at least a few by name. I owe a special debt to Hyun Soo Kil, who was my senior Korean administrator my first two years in Korea, during the early months of which I firmly resisted adapting to Korea. I know that I must have embarrassed him hundreds of times, and I am especially sorry to have lost track of him over the years because he is probably unaware that I made any progress at all toward learning to think Korean.

And I especially want to thank my Korean "mother" and "father," Dr. and Mrs. Hyun Kyu Hwan. He was director of the Korean Red Cross office in Seoul during our first stay in Korea. My wife and I will never forget their generosity and their loving efforts to make us respectable enough to be their American "son" and "daughter."

My thanks also go to my friend and colleague George Renwick, who first asked me to write this book for the InterAct Series around 1980; to my longtime editor and friend, David Hoopes, who kept hounding me until I finally agreed to write it fifteen years later (and who contributed so much in editing the manuscript that we can appropriately call it a mutual effort and together be proud of it); to Judy Carl-Hendrick for her diligence in the final editing of the book, and who unquestionably has improved a thousandfold the manuscript I delivered to her; to Patty Topel for her design of the book and the cover; and to Toby Frank, president of Intercultural Press, who is one of the most helpful people I know, always willing to share her abundant knowledge and encouragement.

Thanks too to my wife's and my good friend, Helen Tieszen, whose many years as professor of the Department of Childhood Development at Yonsei University and as former president of the Korea branch of the Royal Asiatic Society taught her much about learning to think Korean. I particularly thank her for sharing with me her deep knowledge of, and respect for, Koreans.

In Korea, over many years, Dr. Kim Suk San, director of the Korea Welfare Foundation, and Dr. Chi Yang Chin, a professor in the Department of Social Welfare at Chung Ang University, have labored tirelessly to locate financial support for my Korean research. Their personal faith in me has done much to keep my interest in Korea as alive today as it was when it began, more than half a century ago.

Throughout the writing of the manuscript, I have sought the constant advice of my colleague and friend Jin-Kyu (Henry) Joung in making sure that my judgments are not exaggerated and in providing current validation to my interpretation of reality. I turned to Steve Bowen, who has resided and worked in Korea for seven years and is currently Senior

Consultant with Burson-Marsteller in Seoul, for his help in describing the modernization of Korean values, to ensure that they are up-to-the-minute. He has done a superb job of fulfilling that assignment.

I am deeply indebted to Dr. Horace H. Underwood (a lifetime, third-generation resident of Korea), who is currently executive director of the Korean-American Educational Commission, which oversees the Fulbright Program in Korea, and who was formerly the director of the School of Korean Studies at Yonsei University in Seoul, for checking the manuscript for inaccuracies. He made scores of helpful suggestions and corrections, for which I am most grateful. Any mistakes that remain are, of course, mine and not the fault of any of the above consultants.

I have learned much from all of them, but I have learned most from my wife, Norma, who has shared with me a deep and abiding love for the Korea of yesterday, for Korea before it was transformed by the modern Western world, in the days when things were simpler there and much poorer, but much more genuine, too.

Some Facts about Korea

If a poll had been taken in 1940, perhaps as many as 98 percent of Americans would not have been able to answer the question "What and where is Korea?" The Korean War (1950–1953) changed that, and the 1988 Olympics, hosted by Seoul, brought international recognition to South Korea. And, of course, in the year 2000 the surprise meeting between Kim Jong Il of the Democratic People's Republic of Korea and President Kim Dae Jung of the Republic of Korea in the south has been the most recent reminder of the reality of the two Koreas and of the desire that they will one day reunite. Even now, Americans know remarkably little about this tiny peninsula that was once so isolated that, until as late as the early twentieth century, it was known as the "Hermit Kingdom."

For at least a couple of decades, all that most Americans knew about Korea was the misinformation channeled into American homes through the popular sitcom M*A*S*H. Its portrayal of the cultural setting was a mishmash of things Chinese, Japanese, and Korean—with Koreans sometimes played by Japanese actors speaking Japanese!

2

Korea is one of the two oldest continuous civilizations in the world,* second only to China. It was the first East Asian country to absorb Chinese culture. Among the Chinese treasures Korea received between the first century B.C. and the fourth century A.D. were its writing system of ideographs, literature, poetry, music, architecture, astronomy, astrology, medicine, metallurgy, the calendar, Taoism, Confucianism, and Buddhism. Korea was the bridge that passed Chinese culture on to Japan, beginning in A.D. 552, the date considered to be the beginning of Japan's historical period.[†]

The Korean language provides us with a clue to the origin of the Korean people, who are not ethnically related to the Chinese. The Korean language is generally considered to belong to the Ural-Altaic language family, originating between the Ural and Altai Mountains of Central Asia (the Koreans are thus related ethnically to the nomadic peoples of Central Asia, who ranged widely in all directions). As such, it is unrelated to Chinese. It *is* related to the Japanese, Mongol, and Manchu languages and is distantly connected to Turkish, Hungarian, and Finnish.

For years, Korean civilization was considered to be nothing more than a provincial offshoot of Chinese culture, because for many centuries it had been a heavy borrower from its larger neighbor, and for the six centuries immediately prior to being subsumed into the Japanese Empire (1910–1945), Korea was under the suzerainty of the Yuan, Ming, and Qing (Ch'ing) Dynasties of China.

Evidence of Korea's native Altaic beginnings has surfaced only relatively recently, but it is overwhelming. It consists of

---

* Mesopotamia, Egypt, and India all have civilizations that predate China, but the later Arab invasions of Mesopotamia and Egypt and the Aryan invasion of India changed the indigenous populations of these countries and the course of their history to such an extent that they are not considered continuous civilizations.
† It is not, however, Korea's earliest influence on Japan.

comma-shaped, stone-carved jewels of Siberian shamanistic origin,[‡] thought to represent bears' claws; early shamanistic legends of Korea's mythical founder, Tan'gun; the so-called "Scythian flying gallop" depictions of galloping horses in the Koguryŏ tombs of ancient Korea; stone dolmens (huge stone burial monuments) of Neolithic origin; and pre-Buddhist animistic religious rituals (related to Siberian shamanism).

In the eighth century, the capital of the Chinese T'ang Dynasty, Ch'angan (present-day Xian), was the largest city in the world, closely followed by the Korean capital of Kyŏngju, with more than a million citizens. Most Americans are unaware that today Seoul is one of the dozen largest cities in the world.

Contrary to what Americans and Europeans are taught in school, Johannes Gutenberg did not invent movable metal type. The Koreans did, two hundred years before Gutenberg's time. The earliest recorded date for Korean moveable bronze type is A.D. 1234, but its invention is quite possibly even earlier. (Gutenberg did invent the press that holds the type bed, speeding up the printing process.)

Koreans have long been painfully aware that geography has determined the country's fate. Korea is situated on a small peninsula[§] in the midst of larger, more powerful neighbors—China, Russia, and Japan. Koreans speak of being a "shrimp among whales," and they say, "When the whales play, the shrimp get their backs broken."

Seoul is almost equidistant from Beijing, Tokyo, and Vladivostok (about seven hundred miles from each). Because of this precarious position, Korea has, throughout its history, been the recipient of continual intimidation, long periods of

---

[‡] Best known in the literature by their Japanese name *magatma*, having been found in prehistoric Japanese burials, though they were introduced into Japan from Korea probably in the fifth century A.D.

[§] South Korea is often compared in size to Indiana and both South and North together, to Idaho.

foreign domination, and frequent and ominous threats to its existence.

Korea has been forced to be a buffer between the great powers of China, Japan, Russia, and the United States, and invading armies have often trampled Korean soil: the Mongol invasions (1234, 1274, 1281), the invasions of the Japanese warlord Hideyoshi (1592–1598), and the Manchu invasions (1627, 1636). It was forcefully absorbed into the Japanese Empire in 1910 and not freed until the end of World War II.

Until the mid-1960s, Korea was one of the poorest, least developed countries in the world. No one expected the "economic miracle" that would enable Korea to become the first of the Four Little Dragons (sometimes called "Four Little Tigers") of Asia to develop into a major world economy (Taiwan, Hong Kong, and Singapore are the other three).

In 1986, *Forbes* magazine made the surprising prediction that in twenty years South Korea would become one of four new nations to rise to leadership in the world's economy.[11] In November 1994, the *Economist* in Britain shocked its readers when it suggested that by the year 2020, South Korea would become the seventh largest economy in the world, surpassing those of France, the United Kingdom, Italy, Russia, and Brazil. When projections of Korea's future are presented by such respected sources, they must be seriously considered. This is true despite the economic setback Korea experienced in 1997. In 1996, South Korea was accepted as a member of the Organization for Economic Cooperation and Development, the first Asian nation after Japan to be admitted to this otherwise Western club. Korea's membership is an indication of its status as a fully "developed" country.

Here are some other surprising facts:

- South Korea has only 1 percent of the land area of the United States but has one-sixth as many people, mak-

---

[11] South Korea was the smallest of the four. The others were China, India, and Brazil (*Forbes*, 5 May 1986).

ing it sixteen times more densely populated than the United States

- South Korea has more citizens with Ph.D.s per capita than any other country
- South and North Korea together represent the thirteenth largest ethnic and the sixteenth largest language group in the world

Critical Incidents

Introduction

One of the best ways to attain quick, sharp insights into the nature of a foreign culture and the manner in which you will respond to it in a cross-cultural encounter is to attempt to figure out the meaning of realistic incidents that are similar to what you are likely to experience there. Called "critical incidents" by cross-cultural trainers, they are descriptions of interactions involving clashes or misunderstandings arising out of cultural differences that are very likely to occur.

We ask you, the reader, to assume the role of protagonist in these incidents: imagine yourself in the role of an American on your first overseas assignment with the responsibility for managing the Seoul office of an American-based partner in a Korean-American joint venture. Your task is to analyze, interpret, and/or explain what in each case is causing the clash or misunderstanding.

Then as you read the rest of the book and plumb the intricacies of the Korean personality, the answers will become clearer—and they will be richer and more meaningful by your having puzzled over the critical incidents. The critical incidents are followed by a separate discussion of the meaning of each. They will be referred to from time to time, as they relate to later chapters in the book.

While these incidents did not happen to me personally, they do represent the real experiences of hundreds of Americans I have known, and in Korea you are bound to have scores (if not hundreds!) of experiences so similar to these that you will think I have written them all just for you.

The Incidents

Incident 1: Mr. Choi Deserves a Little Praise

You are the American manager of a Korean-based American multinational company at its office in Seoul. You have been on the job in Seoul for nearly a month, and you are pleased that things no longer seem nearly as strange and foreign as they did when you first arrived. Much of your success in adjusting to your new environment is obviously due to one of your employees, Choi Byung Doo, who has been particularly helpful.

Mr. Choi's helpfulness undoubtedly stems from his familiarity with the English language and with American culture, having spent five years in the United States. He immediately took it upon himself to attend to your every need from the moment he met you at Kimpo Airport. He has been especially helpful in acting as go-between with the other Koreans on your staff, convincing them to accept the changes you have made in office procedures since your arrival. Consequently, you are most grateful to Mr. Choi and are determined to acknowledge all he has done for you. You decide to recognize Mr. Choi at the regular morning meeting with your top office staff. By doing so, you will kill two birds with one stone—you'll make Mr. Choi feel good in front of his peers and give the rest of the staff a model to emulate.

As the first order of business at the next meeting, you proudly announce, "Before we hear the reports from the division chiefs this morning, I have an announcement to make. Since I first arrived in Seoul, one member of the staff here has gone far above and beyond the call of duty, sometimes putting in long extra hours of his own time—without any extra compensation—to help me become adjusted to the environment here...."

As you talk in glowing terms, you glance repeatedly in Mr. Choi's direction. Even before disclosing his name, you want to give everyone an idea who it is you are describing. To your surprise, Mr. Choi, rather than expressing appropriately modest pleasure at the remarks which he and everyone else realize are being directed at him, is displaying what appears to you to be a flushed face and an expression that seems to indicate he is being *reprimanded* rather than praised. Seeing this, you immediately set out to correct his obvious misinterpretation. "Don't be mistaken," you say, "I'm not *criticizing*; I'm *praising*. Your behavior, Mr. Choi, has been in every way exemplary."

To your utter surprise, this only seems to make matters worse. Mr. Choi looks as though he wants to crawl under the table. He seems relieved when Mr. Park, the oldest and senior-ranking official on your staff, interrupts to say, "Forgive me, sir, I am dreadfully sorry to interrupt you, but is it possible for us to move on to our division chiefs' reports? I am so sorry I have to excuse myself in fifteen minutes to attend to a business meeting. I am so sorry...."

You get the message and move on quickly to the reports.

Now, since the meeting, it seems that Mr. Choi is deliberately trying to avoid you, and there is an icy chilling in your relationship with all the division chiefs. Your good intentions have obviously backfired.

As you try to analyze the situation, the only interpretation you can make is that the other division chiefs must be jealous of Mr. Choi having been singled out for praise. But that's your style: good work will be openly praised and bad work straightforwardly criticized. It has always worked in the past.

As you consider the matter more, however, you are still

puzzled. Your analysis doesn't explain Mr. Choi's obviously negative reaction. You would think that at least *he* would be pleased with the praise he has received.

What could be the *real* reason for everyone's negative response?

Incident 2: "Hey, Mister, That's My Cab!"

You have been in Korea about three months, long enough to be shocked by the way Koreans sometimes treat each other.

You have encountered or observed a number of instances of rude public behavior, but one in particular stands out in your memory. You were standing on a busy street in Seoul patiently signaling for a taxi. When one finally pulled up, a Korean businessman suddenly appeared from nowhere, and without so much as a "pardon me," he yanked open the door, jumped in, and rode off.

When it happened two more times, you mentioned the experience in conversations with other American expats and found that they had had the same experience.

What could explain this rude behavior?

Incident 3: "But Why Did You Deliberately Lie to Me?"

You have just discovered that your Korean interpreter and intermediary with your Korean staff, Mr. Lee Bong Gap, has deliberately concealed from you a piece of vital information about a problem your business is experiencing for more than three weeks. He told you several outright lies, and then, when you suspected something was wrong and began asking pointed questions to get to the bottom of the matter, his answers misled you.

The most embarrassing part of the incident is that you only learned about what was going on when one of your friendly competitors, another American manager (who had heard about it from his senior Korean administrator) passed the story along to you.

Now that it is out in the open, you are livid and ready to take action, but what should you do?

Incident 4: Why Can't These People Be More Direct?

Although you had fully intended when you accepted the Korean assignment to learn enough Korean to be able to function on the job in the language, doing so has proven much more difficult than you had anticipated. Consequently, you have been relying on an interpreter most of the time or have tried to communicate directly with some of the braver members of your staff willing to use their less-than-fluent English.

Neither of these solutions is very satisfactory, however, and you feel you never fully understand what is going on (and certainly not the subtle innuendoes). This state of affairs is particularly frustrating because the entire Korean staff seems to look to you to give them the final, authoritative word on every issue. They also seem to feel most comfortable presenting everything to you in the most ambiguous and uncertain terms; yet they expect you, as boss, to be as definitive as possible in giving them precise orders regarding exactly what to do.

You are finally beginning to suspect that whenever someone comes to you with a carefully crafted statement such as "It seems as though it might have been that Mr. Hwang may possibly have told Mrs. Noh that perhaps it was not wise for her to do certain things," what the person is actually trying to say is this: "Mr. Hwang *definitely* told Mrs. Noh not to do that certain thing ever again."

Such extreme indirectness is driving you crazy. "Why can't these people say what they mean? Why don't they tell me about potentially dangerous situations before they happen? Are they intentionally trying to cause me problems?" You doubt any deliberateness, but this constant state of ambiguity is intolerable.

What shall I do? you ask yourself, getting angrier and angrier.

Incident 5: *Caring for People in Need: Insiders and Outsiders*

You were having lunch the other day with Mr. Pak Yoon Goo, a Korean acquaintance you had met through activities at the Seoul Rotary Club. Mr. Pak was talking about his experiences during his three years in the United States, when he said, "The one thing that shocked me most about the U.S. was the poor homeless people on the streets of Washington, D.C. Why, they were right in front of the White House! How is it that in the U.S.—one of the richest countries in the world, a model of democracy, and where you are always accusing other countries of human rights violations—you treat your homeless people so callously?"

You sputtered, trying to find an acceptable answer to a question you had not thought about before, but you could only come up with a reply so lame that it was not even convincing to yourself. "Well, if they really wanted a job, they could find one."

You were surprised by Mr. Pak's accusation, and it made you pause, stirring in you feelings of compassion for people who were probably trapped in their condition in ways you could not fully understand. But the real surprise was yet to come. It occurred a couple of days later, when the two of you were walking together in one of the outlying districts of Seoul. As you approached a subway entrance, you passed an obviously destitute mother with a dirty, ragged, and ill-fed baby. Mr. Pak, apparently having completely forgotten the charge of callousness he had leveled at the United States a few days before, muttered, "Why does she have to impose her ugliness upon us?" In his tone was a curious bitterness, as if by her very presence she had intentionally offended him.

How can you explain the contradiction in Mr. Pak's attitude?

Incident 6: *What's a Friend for?*

Mr. Pak Yoon Goo, your Rotary friend, often makes references to his experiences as a student in the United States years ago. He is puzzled by some of the things he experienced or observed and seems to defy you to justify them.

One recent comment was particularly confusing. "The thing that surprised me most about America is that Americans have no friends," he said, in a somewhat adversarial tone.

"What do you mean?" I countered. "I've just finished addressing nearly three hundred Christmas cards to send out to the friends you accuse me of not having." I wanted the tone of my reply to let him know I had not taken his accusation lying down.

"There you go," he said, with only slightly less antagonism than I had shown. "You Americans think that the hundreds of people you send Christmas cards to are your *friends* and that a card once a year is enough attention to give to a friend."

That last comment really hurt, but before I could reply, he let go with another. "We Koreans say that Americans are peculiar people because they treat their friends like strangers and strangers like friends. It must be true," he said, "because we Koreans often say that very thing." I let this go and simply asked him what he meant by his statement about friends and strangers.

He went on to say, "In Korea, no one has *lots* of friends. Everyone probably has only one or two or, at most, three friends. You can't afford to have more than one or two because you have to give so much to each true friend."

"What do you mean?" I said. "What do you *give* your friends?"

What do you think Mr. Pak replied?

Incident 7: A New Idea from America

Ever since arriving and becoming familiar with procedures in your new office, you had been puzzled as to why your predecessor, Mr. Jones, had not initiated a performance review process. You learned a long time ago that such reviews are critical to effective management.

Since you realized that Koreans expect "top-down" managerial procedures, you decided to begin by assigning your top managers the task of writing an evaluation of each of their immediate subordinates. Simultaneously, you told them of your intent to first write an evaluation for each of them so as to provide a model for them to use in their own assessments. Then, right on down to the first-line supervisors, each successive level would write evaluations of their immediate supervisees.

At the next meeting of top-level staff you announced the plan with confidence and enthusiasm, referring to it as a "new idea from America." You detected some slight resistance, but no more, you felt, than announcing such a plan would generate in an American office setting. You assured them that everyone, including yourself, would be involved and that training seminars would be offered to help them master the procedures. In addition, you emphasized the importance of not being "too glowing" in evaluating employees, one aim of which was to identify areas needing improvement. "After all," you said, "nobody's perfect." You also told them you had several other "little ideas" from America you were planning to put in place to help the office function more effectively.

Although you had been on the job in Korea less than a year, you felt as though you knew each of your top managers well enough to give them an honest, fair, and accurate evaluation. The evening dinner and drinking sessions had been especially helpful in getting to know them, and you felt you could be direct in your assessment.

You assured them of the absolute privacy of all the evaluations and emphasized repeatedly that the purpose of putting negative comments into the evaluation was not to insult or punish employees for wrongdoing, but to indicate areas in which they, even the best of them, could strive to improve. In spite of these efforts and a training workshop conducted by a new Seoul training company using up-to-date U.S. training methods, the evaluations written by the top-level managers about their subordinates included absolutely no negative comments, even for employees you knew deserved them. Quite annoyed, you have now decided to call in Mr. Cho, manager of the production division, to discuss why he failed to mention the flagrantly poor performance of one of his staff.

How do you expect Manager Cho to justify himself? What aspects of an American-style performance review process do you think might be less appropriate in Korean culture than in U.S. culture?

Incident 8: Bribery and Nepotism

During nearly a year in Korea you have encountered numerous examples of bribery or suspected bribery, graft, corruption (including embezzlement), and enough examples of nepotism to almost turn you off from doing further business there. You are also aware that your Korean staff has actually shielded you from many of the most blatant examples of these practices either by not reporting them or by lying to you to cover them up.

You have made your feelings clear about these evils and have stated unequivocally that if you ever uncover any cases of bribery, graft, or kickbacks in your company, you will fire the responsible person on the spot, no questions asked and no severance pay given, regardless of the company's severance policy.

For you, as for many Americans, these are issues to which you react with strong emotions—and often self-righteousness—and which you perceive as being rife with legal land mines.

Laying ethics and morality aside for a moment, consider as many reasons as you can why people—in this case Koreans—would want to ask for or pay a bribe. What is the difference between a bribe and a tip? Are there any conceivable advantages to the practice of nepotism in the workplace?

Incident 9: "You're Fired, Mr. Lim!"

One of your midlevel employees, Mr. Lim, has deliberately and regularly disobeyed direct orders you have given him. The last time he did so, you told him, in no uncertain terms, that you would fire him if he ever failed to follow orders again. And now he's done it again.

You intend to waste no time carrying out your threat. But just as you are about to do so, his superior, Mr. Koh, comes to you to represent Mr. Lim and to argue on his behalf. While your initial reaction is one of annoyance because you want to get on with the firing, you take the time to listen to Mr. Koh's argument, which is that you should be more lenient with Mr. Lim and take a more deliberate course of action. You argue that Mr. Lim has had his chance, and firing is the only course left to you, since you had given him adequate warning and an ultimatum. Mr. Koh persistently appeals to your beneficence, and not your logic, and you finally become so exasperated that you say, "Okay, Mr. Koh, please tell me how *you* would handle this situation."

What are some of the suggestions Mr. Koh might offer in response?

Incident 10: "I Hate to Tell You, Sir, but You Don't Act Like a Boss"

Koreans use drinking parties after hours to get to know each other more intimately and to facilitate working together. During the workday itself, relationships are formal, even ritualistic. The drinking party provides a means of lubricating these relationships and facilitating the development of closer interaction within the group. In this context Koreans often use the excuse of alcohol to allow them to say things—without penalty—that would be too rude to say in other circumstances or that would, in normal interactions, cause a loss of face. The idea is that a person who is drunk cannot be held responsible for his actions.

All of this is a prelude to your own painful but useful experience after you had been a manager in Korea for almost a year. It happened one night at such an after-hours drinking party, which by then you had grown used to attending once or twice a week (rather than every night as your Korean staff does). After much drunken revelry, one of your normally quiet, respectful employees said, in a voice loud enough to stop all the rest of the conversation, "But sir, you don't act like a boss!"

This may not seem, in print and from an American perspective, a serious charge, but for you it was like a kick in the stomach. You had been striving during the year to meet your own expectations in addition to those of your Korean colleagues, trying to be as effective a manager as possible. You were stunned, but you forced a laugh. Moments later the Koreans were laughing in relief. You had passed the test and gotten the message. By laughing, you had also saved their faces so that you were still good friends. For that moment, nothing else was needed.

The next day, however, you met with Mr. Kim Doo Oon, another Rotarian friend, in private. On several past occasions he had allowed you to take him into your confidence in clarifying what you had done wrong in several embarrassing situations.

You had been in Korea long enough to learn a secret that is worth the price of a round-trip ticket from Chicago to Seoul: you can get any Korean to level with you if, *in private*, you precede your question with the phrase "truthfully speaking" (*"sasheel"* or *"sasheel-un"* or *"sasheel-dero"*). With that magic phrase, and the cover of privacy, and having Mr. Kim serve in the capacity of "cultural informant" on other occasions, you were able to draw from him a flood of examples of "ways in which you weren't acting like a manager" in Korean eyes.

What might some of those ways have been?

Discussion of the Incidents

Incident 1: Mr Choi Deserves a Little Praise

The main point of this case is that it is just as embarrassing to Koreans to be *praised* publicly as it is to be reprimanded publicly. The old Asian proverb (often misattributed to Confucius) applies to Koreans as well as to the Japanese and Chinese to whom it is more generally attributed. "The nail that sticks out gets pounded in." Koreans are group-oriented and anything that makes an individual stand out removes that person from the group. Both praise and criticism should be given privately. In a business setting it is also best to consider Korean workers as members of teams, with praise or rewards given to or shared by the entire group.

This incident also underlines the importance of identifying a Korean informant who can explain things to you from the Korean point of view. Be careful in making your choice, for once you have offered such signs of favor or friendship, it is not easy to withdraw your friendship without hurting the other person unduly (i.e., making him or her lose face).

Sometimes the first Koreans to approach you and offer their help may have ulterior motives for doing so. They may want to "use" you to their advantage. Mr. Choi, in this critical incident, is clearly not befriending you for his own advancement. But someone else might just as easily have been out to feather his or her own nest.

Incident 2: "Hey Mister, That's My Cab!"

Koreans assign overriding importance to whether someone is a member of their ingroup or not and then treat the person accordingly.

Ingroups may be blood relatives, schoolmates, classmates, or members of the same organization. Those who belong to your ingroup are treated with respect and concern. Those who are not are invisible; they are nonentities. Koreans think of them as "unpersons." A stranger waiting for a cab is such an unperson toward whom no moral or social obligation is felt.

Americans will donate blood to save the lives of unknown strangers at some abstract future date. Koreans find this difficult to understand. On the other hand, a Korean would be willing to give virtually all of his or her blood to a close friend in need of it—the sense of obligation is that great.

Ingroup and outgroup attitudes are discussed extensively in chapter 8. It is an issue that needs to be understood and carefully considered before one passes judgment.

In the future our expat could avoid having his cab stolen out from under him by catching a taxi at a nearby large hotel, or if he is in his office, by asking one of his junior staff members to hail a taxi for him and bring it to the office door.

Incident 3: *"But Why Did You Deliberately Lie to Me?"*

Koreans have traditionally found it difficult to say no or tell an unpleasant truth to a superior. It is even more difficult to do so with a foreigner, and Koreans will often tell a pleasant lie rather than an unpleasant truth. They consider doing so similar to what Americans call telling a "white lie," even when the extent of their lie far exceeds the limits of an American white lie.

This is done not to deceive but to *protect* the other person's *kibun* (sense of well-being) or to save his own or the other's face. (Kibun and face are discussed in depth in chapter 6.)

In practical terms, this means that when a Korean says yes, it does not always mean what yes means to us. It may simply mean "I would rather say yes even though I don't mean yes, than make you angry or cause you unhappiness." It may also mean "I hear what you have said but I don't agree with it."

However, if Mr. Lee is going to serve as your interpreter and intermediary, he is going to have to modify his operating style. This will not be easy for him to do. It will also be necessary for you to modify yours. Your anger will only exacerbate the situation, so first, calm down and realize he is only responding in the polite Korean way (out of respect for you), and it will take some time (and much patience on your part) for him to learn to be more truthful in reporting unpleasant situations to you. Any sign of anger from you will only make it all the more impossible for him to be straightforward.

Rumors spread rapidly in Korea, and you should not be mortified, or even unduly concerned, to learn from a competitor about a subject on which you were being kept in the dark about. Rumors should be considered a tactful way of getting a truthful message to a person in an indirect, and therefore appropriate, way. They are a main source of information in Asian societies and should be valued accordingly.

Incident 4: Why Can't These People Be More Direct?

Even Koreans who speak fluent English may still find it difficult to communicate with you in English, because the nature of the Korean language is to be intentionally less direct, less specific, and more ambiguous than English-speaking people tend to be. Therefore, for a Korean to translate Korean into English, he or she has to do much more than simply translate the words. Koreans find it more acceptable to hint at or suggest something rather than to be crystal clear in their communication. This generalization becomes especially true when it is obvious that someone is responsible for having done something wrong and is, therefore, susceptible to losing face for what he or she has done. And for the American to press for the specifics that will reveal the painful truth also puts the interpreter as well as the speaker in an embarrassing position.

This becomes even more critical when the American with whom the Korean speaker is communicating is likely to be overquick to respond angrily, to identify the culprit, and then to display his or her anger openly, for all to witness.

Koreans will often pass on a rumor in indefinite and uncertain terms, such as "It seems as though it might be that so-and-so possibly happened...." The reason for stating it in this way is to make sure you will get the information but the speaker will not be accused of having been the one who told you.

The prudent foreigner operating in Korea will, therefore, have to learn to become less quick to anger and less condemning when he or she discovers something that is potentially upsetting. Learning to control your anger and to respond more calmly and not to display your emotions is the way to proceed. (It is also one of the subtle ways that establishes one's status as a true "gentleman" or "gentlelady.")

Koreans tend to think of Americans to whom everything is seen as a "crisis" and who display their raw emotions at the drop of a hat like immature young children instead of adults who have gained composure and who have learned to control and mask their emotions, rather than allowing their emotions to control them.

It is not surprising how learning such control, and especially how learning to keep your anger in check, makes for a much less stressful life—in the United States, incidentally, as well as in Korea.

Incident 5: Caring for People in Need: Insiders and Outsiders

Mr. Pak sees no relationship between the two events because he is judging neither of them as instances where someone is in need and, therefore, one ought to feel sorry for them. Instead, he is judging them from the impression they are likely to make on the observer.

In the case of the homeless in America, Mr. Pak is not feeling sorry for them because they have no home to live in. Instead, he is judging and blaming the American people, or the American government, because they seem not to care that while they could easily afford to give the homeless a place to live (or at least prevent them from occupying the prime real estate in front of the White House) in order to keep from giving foreigners an unfavorable image of America, they choose not to. He wonders how we could not be aware of the unfavorable image we are giving of our country.

In the case of Mr. Pak's response to the poor Korean mother and child, he has no compassion for her because she is not a part of any of his own "ingroups." Therefore, he feels no personal responsibility for her well-being. Instead, he is concerned that your seeing her may give you an unfavorable impression of Korea.

Incident 6: What's a Friend for?

Mr. Pak probably replied, "Everything." Koreans define a friend as a person you can call at three o'clock in the morning with a request for money and the friend will come, bringing the money, without even asking why you are calling at this unusual hour or what you need the money for. A friend is a person to whom you feel a total and unreserved obligation; therefore, Koreans identify very few people as friends.

Most of the people Americans call friends are, from the Korean point of view, acquaintances, but as Americans, we tend to consider everyone a "friend" from the moment we meet. Compared with Koreans, Americans are reluctant to sacrifice time or money, even for people we consider friends.

One key lies in Mr. Pak's comment that "Americans are peculiar people because they treat their friends like strangers and strangers like friends." The obligation Americans feel toward friends is far less than what Koreans feel, and the obligations toward strangers are much greater.

Incident 7: A New Idea from America

Because of the significant differences between what is considered reasonable and appropriate in the United States and in

Korea, you should expect there to be major differences in evaluating performance. Such reviews, while not exactly awaited with open arms by American employees either, are at least accepted as a reasonable requirement, since our society bases salaries and promotions on merit rather than on longevity.

In Korea, where saving face is seen as more important than any other interpersonal requirement, the last thing any courteous person is permitted to do is to say something negative to another person's face. If an unfavorable comment is ever called for, etiquette requires that either it be hinted at so lightly that no American would be likely to catch its meaning or that it be conveyed in privacy by an intermediary.

This being the case, it should be obvious that performance evaluations—especially those requiring negative as well as positive comments—would certainly not fit comfortably into the Korean culture.

Even though your job description gives you the authority to do so, you would be wise not to make drastic changes within your first year in Korea, before you have had enough time to familiarize yourself with Korean customs. Even then, you would be wise to run the idea past several of your own compatriots in country to get their responses before initiating such potentially inappropriate reforms.

The first question asked in Critical Incident 7 is "How do you expect Manager Cho to justify himself (for not having included an account of his supervisee's negative action)?" Given the rules of Korean etiquette, recalling that the American manager is Mr. Cho's immediate supervisor, Manager Cho is unlikely to offer anything at all in his own defense— except to say nothing and to lower his flushed face in shame before his superior—but he will certainly find it difficult to comprehend why this foreigner in such a position of authority does not understand the rules of etiquette (which Manager Cho, in all likelihood, considers universal rather than Asian). Nor will he understand why the American manager wants this person to lose still more face, long after the specific violation, whatever it was, has been punished and forgotten. Why, he will now wonder, must it be brought up all over again? Does he want this employee to leave the company in utter humiliation? And, ultimately, how inhumane does this American want others to think he is?

Besides, Manager Cho knows, even though the American has promised that the written evaluations will be "absolutely private," that once committed to writing, such negative comments could eventually become widely circulated in Korea, and his unfortunate employee's negative evaluation would become the "gossip of the week."

There are some American ideas that simply will not work in Korea, and the truthful, balanced evaluation report probably heads the list.

Undoubtedly the most threatening thing that the American said, as he explained the idea behind the American performance evaluation process, was that he had several other new ideas from America that he was planning to introduce later.

Incident 8: Bribery and Nepotism

Bribery and nepotism are common in Korea, much more so than in the United States. In fact they are two of the most common Korean practices that most Westerners find hardest to tolerate. The basic difference is that Koreans consider them more acceptable. Korean bureaucrats and teachers have traditionally been paid such low salaries that bribes have been necessary for them to survive and are considered by many a kind of service fee or a tip for services rendered (or yet to be rendered). While it is true, by and large, that small bribes are no longer needed to convince low-level officials to do their job, such bribes are still given to hasten the decision-making process. It is also true that large bribes are still too often given to high-level officials.

The main difference between a "bribe" and a "reward" is

that the former is given before the desired service and the latter is given after. From the Korean point of view, giving a reward instead of a bribe is tantamount to saying you don't trust the other person to deliver until you have the goods in hand.

As for nepotism, it goes hand in hand with the emphasis Koreans place on ingroup/outgroup feelings: you can trust a blood relative but not an outsider. From their point of view, it is therefore desirable to place relatives in positions around you. As a manager in Korea, I soon learned that hiring a person who had been recommended by someone who was already in my employ often meant nepotism was involved; nevertheless, it has the built-in advantage of providing me with a ready-made "go-between" should the new employee need to be reprimanded for a wrongdoing.

Incident 9: "You're Fired, Mr. Lim!"

Considering the fact that you are Mr. Koh's supervisor, it is highly unlikely that he will aggressively take Mr. Lim's defense in replying directly to your specific question of what he would do. To do that would certainly imply, in Mr. Koh's mind, direct criticism of his own boss, for it would carry the insinuation that you don't know how to be a good manager if you don't even know how to properly handle a disobedient employee.

But if he were to answer honestly, his answer would undoubtedly be more involved than the one simple step you have in mind—an immediate termination of Mr. Lim. It would also be much more likely to contain many of the steps discussed later in chapter 12, undoubtedly involving a Korean intermediary who would act on your direct behalf. As well, his actions may likely include having Mr. Lim write a letter of apology to be placed in his personnel file and, as a subsequent step, temporarily reassigning the wayward employee to an unpopular provincial branch office far from home, at least once or twice, until the employee finally comes to the realization that it would be better for him to quit than to move one more time.

Even then, you should not be surprised if, just before Mr. Lim quits, Mr. Koh suggests that you award Mr. Lim a certificate for his "many years of faithful service to the company" as a parting gesture and as a means of allowing Mr. Lim to save face in his community.

Incident 10: "I Hate to Tell You, Sir, but You Don't Act Like a Boss"

Before we answer the question posed at the end of Critical Incident 10 [How might you have not acted like a (Korean) boss?], let's point out some of the things you did *right* in your response to the criticism you received in the after-hours drinking party. Your intuitive response of laughter, even though it was a forced (rather than a genuine) response, was precisely the right one—and very Korean. Remember, Koreans believe that anyone acting under the influence of alcohol cannot be held responsible for his action, no matter how rude or embarrassing it might be. You should also remember not to show, in future interactions with the employee who made the uncomplimentary comment, even the slightest trace of resentment. If anything, you should go out of your way to give little signs that everything is normal between you.

In his "frank" response to your direct request for helpful information, Mr. Kim Doo Oon would most likely frame his comments as if he were describing the actions of numerous *other* American managers he had observed rather than being descriptive of *your* style, but you would be able to recognize your all-too-American drive for equality and your compulsion to come across as "just one of the boys" rather than playing the role of someone who is a superior supervising inferiors.

This is the list of behaviors that Mr. Kim would probably cite, based on how he had seen many other American bosses acting inappropriately toward their Korean employees.

- They act as though they are just one of the employees and not their superior and their boss.

- They are too friendly to everybody.

- They are always smiling at everybody, even those in the lowest positions, and talking to them in language that would normally be used among close friends.

- They freely admit to their underlings that there are many things (especially in the Korean context) that they do not know—and they often display this (perhaps unconsciously) by asking their employees questions that any and every boss ought to know the answers to—otherwise, why would they be the boss?

- They are often too direct—too blunt—and straightforward in their comments.

- Their direct orders are often framed as questions, for example, "Would you mind doing this for me?" This seems to Koreans to demonstrate weakness.

- Americans say too many "thank yous" for things Korean employees should be doing as a regular part of their job.

- Americans are often openly critical of the Korean way of doing things, and even when they are not directly critical, they seem to be critical when they are constantly telling their Korean employees "the way we do it in America"—as if that is obviously the superior way.

- They often become openly emotional—by being either too childishly happy over something or too severely condemning (in a highly overwrought, passionate way) of some particular Korean practice (like bribery, for instance). Why should they become so exercised by it?

Another point that Mr. Kim could make is that Korean managers take more interest in their employees' personal lives than their American counterparts normally do. It is not extraordinary, for example, for a Korean manager to pay a personal visit to the sick wife of one of his laborers, who is in the hospital. (See also the comments on page 170.)

This incident also makes the secondary point that every Westerner who wants to adapt to the Korean way of thinking and performing while in Korea *must* have at least one trusted Korean informant who can explain things Korean in ways a Westerner can understand.

3

Influence of Asian Religious and Ethical Systems

This chapter examines the philosophical and ethical-religious systems that have provided the values and the rituals that have shaped and enriched Korean culture and given it remarkable stability over a long span of time. One by one, we will consider four major systems and how they have shaped Korean society. In every instance, their influence goes far beyond the spiritual content, affecting other aspects of society.

Taoism

As a religion, Taoism (pronounced "Daoism") is no longer practiced in Korea, but its influence is still felt. Taoism is the least known of the world's major religions, since it never moved substantially outside the East Asian sphere. Taoism is still practiced as a religion in Hong Kong and Taiwan but only in a relatively debased form. It is now heavily infused with superstition and fortune-telling and, most commonly, so thoroughly incorporated into Buddhism that the two are practically indistinguishable. Nevertheless, some familiarity with Taoism is useful because of the strong influence its original philosophy and symbolism have had on Korean life and thought, an influence still evident in present-day Korea.

The founder of Taoism was Lao-tzu, who is thought to have lived in the sixth century B.C. and to have been about fifty years older than Confucius. The principal scripture of Taoism is the Tao Te Ching (pronounced "Da DuhJing"), which has become the most frequently translated book from Chinese into English and which is especially popular among New Age Americans.

Taoism strongly influenced two institutions that have survived and that, unlike religious Taoism, are flourishing: Zen Buddhism and classical Sumi painting. Zen Buddhism is known as Sŏn in Korean (Chan in Chinese, Zen in Japanese). While the content of Zen is Buddhist, its spirit is Taoist. In fact, the description of Taoism which follows may sound familiar to those who know Zen well. Classical Sumi painting is the purest, most respected form of Chinese painting. The austere, black-and-white style was first developed in the Song (Sung) Dynasty but grew directly out of the philosophy of Taoism. It could, in fact, accurately be called Taoism in its visual form. There are Asian artists today still painting in classical Sung style, though they are not as plentiful as they were during the eleventh and twelfth centuries.

The word Tao means the way, the path, or the road. By implication it signifies the way of Nature and, as such, deals with the mystical principle that activates the universe and all things in it. Lao-tzu taught that we should learn from Nature and look to Nature as our teacher. This involves, first, some unlearning. We are advised to stop struggling against Nature and fit ourselves quietly into its flow. Instead of trying to dominate Nature (as Westerners, especially Americans, are inclined to do*), Taoism advocates that we should live by the

---

* In the very first chapter of Genesis, God gives Adam and Eve control over all the animals He has created, and Westerners have not stopped trying to control things since that time.

principle of Wu Wei, which literally means "do nothing." Especially in those situations that are tense or potentially conflict creating, to take no action at all is sound advice, and it is this tendency that is responsible for creating the sense of calmness and the gentleness that we associate with the Asian personality. All we have to do, according to Taoist teaching, is to realize that by our very existence we are an indispensable part of nature. There is nothing further required of us.

The South Korean flag displays one of the most ancient Taoist symbols—the yin-yang circle (*ŭm-yang* or *tae-gŭk*) divided by a gentle S shape, surrounded by four of the sixty-four hexagrams associated with Taoist beginnings. (See Appendix B for more on the Korean flag and the sixty-four hexagrams.) The circle in which these two curved shapes fit is the perfect geometric form, having neither visible beginning nor end and being absolutely identical in every arc of its circumference.

When Western audiences are asked what the symbolic meaning of the yin-yang form is, they invariably answer that the two shapes represent sets of opposing elements. As Westerners, our minds are quick to think of dozens of opposites which are represented by the yin and yang. While this is true as far as it goes, the full meaning or impact of yin-yang is the perfect unity of those apparent opposites within the single, unified circular form; in other words, it is the *unity of the elements that is the important message, not their opposition.*

Yin Represents	Yang Represents
Female energy	Male energy
Passivity	Action
Darkness	Light
Negativeness	Positiveness
Softness	Hardness
Coldness	Warmness
Dampness	Dryness

Yin and yang qualities are best explained to the Western mind by comparing them with the positive and negative charges of electricity. In that context, negative does not mean bad; on the contrary, both forces are equal, and both are absolutely necessary in order for electricity to exist.

Taoism also teaches that there are no such things as animate and inanimate objects, as we in the West suppose. Instead, all things are infused with a living spirit (Ch'i in Chinese; Ki in Korean). This living spirit is sometimes translated as "vital force," "vital energy," or "breath of life," and it fills the mountains, rocks, and trees as well as everything else in the world. It animates every human being, too, and depending on whether we happen to be male or female, we are filled with either yang or yin spirit—yin if female, yang if male. The mountains and the trees, for example, are filled with yang spirit, while the clouds and the air and the water are full of yin energy, all of which provides a clue to how, according to Taoist understanding, people fit into Nature. In order to give our yin or yang energy to Nature, we need merely to be and to realize that we are an indispensable part of Nature, contributing to its full measure of yinness and yangness. It means, too, that while it is impossible for us to dominate Nature, our yinness or yangness is absolutely necessary in order to complete the balance of Nature. Ch'i is, after all, the invisible force that energizes the universe.

Water has become the perfect Taoist symbol. It is soft and yielding; it easily conforms to the shape of whatever vessel is provided to contain it. Yet, that very same water is so powerful and so persistent that it can cut through the hardest, most impenetrable rock. Be like the water, Taoism urges us.

Ideal Taoists are absolutely calm and composed at all times because they are at peace with the world and in harmony with themselves. They are unpretentious, humble, quiet, and confident. They accept what is as what should be. They lead simple lives; their needs are few. They do not run around frantically chasing their tails, but are comfortable and at ease with themselves, content to simply do nothing when they are doing nothing. Their approach to living is nonimposing, noncontrolling, nonmanipulative.

Geomancy,[†] the ancient Asian art of placing graves and buildings in the landscape so that they will have the most propitious effect, also grew out of Taoism, as did the *I Ching* (the *Book of Changes*),[‡] a method of reading future events as well as affecting their causation. The Chinese concept of the sixty-four hexagrams, the Five Elements (wood, fire, earth, metal, and water), and the Chinese myths of the Eight Immortals (and their search for the special peach, which would give its lucky finders immortality) also grew out of Taoism.

Lao-tzu was very clear in stating that the person who claims to be able to define or explain Taoism must be considered a charlatan at best, for it is truly ineffable. The remarkable thing, however, is that it is almost as difficult to identify the specific ways in which Taoism shows itself in present-day Korean society as it is to define Taoism itself. Part of the problem lies in the fact that, whatever little remains today of Taoism as a religion, it has either been subsumed into Buddhism or is claimed as a part of Confucianism.

Besides Zen and Sumi, the most obvious way Taoism survives in Korea is in the description of the Ideal Taoist, although it, too, has been obscured by the idea of the Confucian Gentleman (described below) because of the way the two have blended so harmoniously. In actuality, nothing could be further apart than the rule-bound Confucian Gentleman and the rule-free, philosophical, and reflective Ideal Taoist. It is only the skill with which they have been joined that makes them seem so compatible and so "natural." One

---

[†] Geomancy has become known in English by its Chinese name—*feng shui* (*pungsu* in Korean).

[‡] Many "New Agers" frequently mispronounce it as "eye-ching", but the correct pronunciation is "ee jing." The *I Ching* is often mistakenly attributed to Confucius.

other way in which Taoism remains alive lies in the manner in which Koreans relate to Nature, especially Nature on the grand scale of, say, the Grand Canyon. Former Korean president Kim Young Sam[§] has said that the reason he likes to go hiking in the mountains is that it "allows him to empty his mind." It is also reflected in the general calmness Koreans display in the graceful acceptance of that which they cannot control. When one has succeeded in controlling one's ego, one no longer needs to feel threatened by the forces of life.

Confucianism

Kung Fu Tze, whose name was latinized to "Confucius" by early Jesuit scholars, was, until Mao Tse Tung (Mao Zedong), the only Chinese whose name most Americans recognized. Until Mao proclaimed him to be an "enemy of the people," Confucius clearly had a greater effect on the lives of Asia's millions than any other single person.

During his lifetime, Confucius, many have fantasized, engaged in an ongoing public argument with Lao-tzu as to the best path for society to follow. Even though they were contemporaries, there is no evidence they ever met. Each proposed a way of life in drastic contrast to the other's. Confucius' way was the more conservative, formalized, and rigid, anchored in the rituals of everyday life. His teachings were full of rules, rituals and ceremonies, ancestor veneration, filial piety, and advice on the proper relationships between people of unequal rank and position (see chapter 7 for an extensive discussion of this aspect of Korean culture). He abhorred corruption in government, and he had amazing success with his demand that public servants live by the highest moral standards. To Confucius, the ideal man was the Gentleman Scholar (also called "landed gentry" or "the literati" in Chi-

---

[§] The "Sam" in his name is correctly pronounced "Sahm," not as in the nickname for Samuel.

nese writings), who lived off his land holdings and never engaged in manual labor of any kind. The only professions he was permitted to engage in were those of bureaucrat, professor/scholar, or military strategist of the highest rank. That admonition, plus Confucius' insistence that bureaucrats live by a code of absolute morality, has resulted in bureaucrats, despite contemporary instances of graft and bribery, receiving significantly more respect and even admiration than bureaucrats elsewhere normally do.

But most often a member of the landed gentry pursued no specific occupation and could best be described by what we refer to as the Renaissance Man, or perhaps more precisely translated, the "Superior Man,"[11] broadly capable in a wide range of intellectual, aesthetic, and professional pursuits. Historically, the ideal Confucian Gentleman (in Korean tradition, the person of highest rank in society) had land that provided sufficient income for living well, with plenty of servants, and without his ever having to do any physical labor. Instead, he could devote his time to pursuing the arts—calligraphy, painting, poetry—and his broader interest in scholarship.

The Confucian Gentleman found it as easy to philosophize as to engage in planning military strategy, teaching disciples, serving in the bureaucracy, or performing the rituals of ancestor worship. These superior men, especially the bureaucrats, became the "priests" of what evolved into the Confucian religion, performing for their communities the ubiquitous rituals that their strict beliefs constantly required.

Confucian values (see below) dictated and were reflected by the gentleman scholar's life situation and personal demeanor, characterized by decorum, propriety, and calmness. Never would this superior person display his emotions publicly. Becoming angry and addressing someone with denigrating words (except toward the lowest of servants) would be

---

[11] In the extremely sexist society of the time they were always men.

the best indication that one was *not* a Confucian Gentleman. In Korean tradition, losing control of your emotions indicates immaturity, certainly not a characteristic of a superior man. Quietness and reserve are always preferred to loquaciousness. His manner is extremely formal. He shows the utmost respect for other people (except when under the occasional influence of alcohol and therefore not considered to be responsible for his actions). Although the scholar-gentleman was expected to be an absolutely moral person, he did not have to give up liquor; indeed, one of his strengths was considered to be his ability to hold his liquor well and outdrink others.

Confucius spelled out precisely which values his followers should live by:

propriety	benevolence
sincerity	reverence
faithfulness	moderation
studiousness	calmness
justice	truth-seeking

These were known as the Confucian virtues. To these, the *Hsiao Ching*¶ added several others: filial piety, loyalty, observance of rituals, moral virtue, deference to those in authority, and self-discipline.

In addition to these values, it was important that societal harmony be maintained at all times and at any cost. One must be vigilant not to let chaos reign but rather to eliminate it the moment one perceives the slightest evidence of its existence. Here Confucianism was in accord with the Chinese idea that the emperor had a right to rule only as long as he could maintain the "Mandate of Heaven." Any evidence of chaos in natural phenomena, such as floods, earthquakes, or rivers suddenly changing their course, were interpreted as celestial signs that the emperor had lost the Mandate of

---

¶ The *Hsiao Ching* is the later Confucian classic of Filial Piety.

Heaven and should be removed from office. Any evidence that governmental restrictions were being ignored in the outlying areas, or that mass demonstrations and riots were being allowed, was also seen as signs of loss of the Mandate. This has caused Asian monarchs to rule with an iron hand and move swiftly the moment it seemed the masses were getting out of control.

In the same vein, Confucius felt strongly that the best society was one that was strongly hierarchical and that every human interaction should take into account the inequality of rank of the two (or more) people who were interacting. Age was the principal criterion for determining hierarchical preference, then one's official rank, then gender (with male outranking female), and, finally, the social status of one's family.

Beyond these hierarchical rankings of superiority, however, all people were always to be treated with civility and in ways that would protect their integrity and human dignity. To act in such a manner was itself a mark of one's own superior upbringing. It was therefore incumbent on one to always act in ways that placed primary importance on saving the other person's face as well as one's own. Face is of such importance in all East and Southeast Asian countries, and the causes of loss of face are sometimes so different from those in the United States that this subject is discussed in considerable depth in chapter 6.

The Civil Service Examination of China is the oldest in the world, starting in the Han Dynasty (which lasted from the third century B.C. to the third century A.D.) and was based on a thorough knowledge of the Confucian classics. For this and other reasons, Confucianism is considered by many to be more a social philosophy than a religion, though it is frequently referred to as "religious humanism," since it addresses certain aspects of human nature and the larger meaning of life in common with the other great religions. No one disputes the fact, however, that it had an enormous impact on the ethics and the social mores of all East Asian cultures.

It is significant that from the fifteenth century to the present, Confucianism has probably held a greater importance in Korea than it did in any other Asian country, including China and Japan. This may have been because the Confucian worldview fits so comfortably into the Korean pattern of accepting hierarchy, structure, and control in life. The Koreans have taken Confucius' teachings, rituals, ceremonies, and prescribed protocol for proper human interaction much more seriously and embodied his values in their attitudes and behaviors much more intentionally than have the people of other Asian countries. Anyone who wants to study Confucianism in daily life today would be well advised to go not to China or Japan, but to South Korea, where Confucianism is still very much alive.

Many of the behaviors, customs, values, personality traits, and common practices described in the remaining chapters of this book grow directly, and with relatively little modification, out of the original principles propounded by Confucius himself (and elaborated on by his most prominent disciple, Mencius) and further crystallized by a half-dozen Chinese scholars who, in the eleventh century, created a Neo-Confucian revival. Chief among these scholars was Chu Hsi, who was particularly idolized in Korea because his articulation of the new rules of Neo-Confucianism were so specific that they left little doubt about how one was to act in every situation and in every relationship. For this reason, Korea, in all aspects except possibly in modern business practices, can be fairly described as an extremely conservative society. There are several obvious areas where Confucian conservatism has left its mark on Korean society. Among them are

Ancestor worship (ancestor veneration)
Funerary rites
Succession and inheritance patterns
Position of women
Institution of marriage
Kinship groups

Social status and rank
Respect for scholar-officials
Confucius described the future in terms of an ideal past, a Golden Age which served as a model to guide behavior then and forever. This entwining of past, present, and future resulted eventually in a cyclical, spiraling concept of time among Asians, a concept that contrasts sharply with the Western belief that time progresses in a straight line, endlessly, into the future. This different viewpoint affects the perceptual orientation of Easterners in ways that often present obstacles to effective communication and interaction with Westerners.

One aspect of Korean culture affected by Confucianism, and one that is significantly different from U.S. culture, is ancestor veneration and the role ancestors are considered to play in one's life. In Korea, the family is composed not only of its living members but also of its deceased members. In fact, in death they are now in a better position to influence your life than when they were living, and, of course, this influence can be for either good or evil. This means one has extra motivation to perform the funerary rituals and the annual observances as well as to employ the best possible geomancer to select the most propitious burial site.

Since the strong Asian sense of filial piety is also Confucian in its origin, the living members of one's extended family to the farthest possible extension of blood relationship hold a very special place of esteem and loyalty.

Respect for the past and its traditions and rituals; for protocol, propriety, and decorum; and for well-established rites of passage such as public ceremonies and memorials, honorary awards, and certificates of appreciation can be directly associated with Confucianism. So can the appreciation of a hierarchical, vertically structured society with clear status demarcations and respect paid to the elderly and to government officials as well as to one's professors, who are venerated all one's life. The scholar-gentleman is still very much alive in Korean society today, particularly among academics and bureaucrats, and the corporate offices of Korea have their share of them also.

Buddhism

Except for the fact that Buddhism is still numerically the dominant religion in Korea and that magnificent Buddhist temples** dot Korea's landscape, the effects of Buddhism on society at large are far fewer and less immediately obvious than are the effects of Confucianism. The reason in part is that Buddhism grew corrupt in the latter half of the Koryŏ Dynasty (918–1392)†† and was ultimately overshadowed by Confucianism. Buddhism in Korea is currently enjoying something of a revival (some are even calling it an "awakening"), with youth groups and rebuilt temples appearing all over South Korea. Buddhism's strength during much of the latter part of the twentieth century was primarily among the poorer classes and older rural women. One reason for its appeal is that it offers the hope of salvation to rich and poor, upper and lower classes alike.

Buddhism began in India as a somewhat austere and ascetic religion (identified as Theravada Buddhism), but it was the more evangelistic strain, Mahayana Buddhism, which took root in East Asian countries, arriving in China (in the

---

** It is in the Buddhist temples that one can get the best feel for what Korean life was like a thousand years ago. The most magnificent temples are farthest from Seoul because when Confucianism replaced Buddhism in the Chosŏn (Yi) Dynasty (1392–1910), the building of Buddhist temples in Seoul, the new capital city, was forbidden.

†† It was this dynasty that gave the West the name by which it identifies Korea to this day. Some speculate that Marco Polo might have carried it back to Europe. Although Marco Polo never visited Korea, there were many Koreans present in the Chinese court of Kubla Khan whom Marco Polo served.

first century A.D.), Korea (in the fourth century), and Japan (carried by Koreans in the sixth century).

The major distinguishing features of Mahayana Buddhism are (1) an emphasis on compassion for all living creatures; (2) the simple, ascetic life its monks are expected to follow; (3) the development of a less difficult path for those who did not wish to pursue the full-time religious path as monks or nuns; and (4) the strong missionary desire of its followers to spread its message to new lands.

Mahayana's emphasis on compassion led to the creation of a new Buddhist entity—the Bodhisattva. A Bodhisattva is one who has earned the right to blissful Nirvana, that is, to Buddahood, and is thereby freed from the endless cycle of birth and rebirth that humans are condemned to as they work through their accumulated karma. However, out of an overwhelming sense of compassion for all sentient creatures, Bodhisattvas have willingly elected to put off Nirvana and, instead, to offer the merit they have stored up to others to help them reach their own Nirvana. In this role, Bodhisattvas are sometimes called "Buddhas of the Future," having put off until some distant future date the enjoyment of the Nirvana they have earned. Thus, the Bodhisattva concept introduced a form of salvation into Mahayana Buddhism that helped increase its popularity.

Buddhism, with its belief in reincarnation (living a series of lives in near-endless succession), has the effect of making death seem less drastic, less final, and therefore, less threatening. The concept of karma, in which the nature of one's next life is determined by one's thoughts and actions in previous lives, puts the ultimate blame for the station of one's birth as well as for the hardships one experiences in each life squarely on one's own shoulders. There is nobody to blame but oneself, and no celestial godhead to look to for salvation. These concepts are difficult for the average Westerner to grasp, but it should be clear that if one were to hold such beliefs, it would result in a substantially different outlook on life. At the very least it would make a person much more accepting of fate, and it would offer an explanation for the catastrophes one often experiences in life. It would also probably make that person somewhat less frantic about accomplishing all that he or she has set out to accomplish, and even less likely to set personal goals to be achieved on one's own.

Traditionally, Asian religions have not been exclusive, and still today, it is not unusual for an Asian to consider him- or herself a Taoist, a Buddhist, and a Confucianist all rolled into one. Modern Korean Christians have, however, inherited the Christian concept of exclusiveness, which causes them to reject such an eclectic gathering of conflicting ideas.

Whether they themselves are Buddhist or not, most Koreans have close relatives who are, so they are familiar with the Buddhist moral code as embodied in the Eight-Fold Path, which proposes eight simple ethical guides to living that it would be difficult for any person of any religion to find objectionable: right belief, right intentions, right speech, right conduct, right livelihood, right effort, right mindfulness, and right concentration.

Worldwide, Buddhism is the fourth largest religion (after Christianity, Islam, and Hinduism). In Korea, there are more people who identify themselves as being Buddhists than members of any other religion.

Christianity

Compared with the other religions we have discussed, Christianity is the newest to have been introduced into Korea, although Catholic missionaries have been active there for more than two hundred years and Protestant missionaries for more than a century.

For many years, the number of Christians in the Korean population was constant at about 11 percent, which was extremely high among Asian countries (with the exception of the Philippines, where Spain implanted Catholicism during its three hundred years of rule). By contrast, Christians make up less than 1 percent of Japan's total population.

Around 1980, for reasons unclear, the number of Korean Christians began to grow rapidly, until by 1992, 25 percent of the population of South Korea were Christian. Korea is also home to the largest Christian church in the world, with a congregation of more than 800,000.

Whatever one's view of missionaries, in Korea one must give them credit for having done much more than spread the Christian gospel. They also introduced Western inventions and technologies, built schools and universities (making modern education available to Koreans), inaugurated equal education for women, introduced Western medicine via medical universities and hospitals, established orphanages, and encouraged the learning of English, which eventually opened graduate-level educational opportunities in Great Britain and the United States to tens of thousands of Korean students.

Foreign missionaries made a major cultural contribution in the resurrection of a phonetic writing system that was first invented in the fifteenth century: *han'gŭl*. Christian missionaries, looking for a simpler medium than Chinese characters (which less-educated Koreans could not read) to use in translating the Bible, were the first to put han'gŭl to extensive use. Today, after four centuries of being ignored, han'gŭl is fully accepted throughout both North and South Korea as the principal medium of written communication. Han'gŭl is considered by many Western linguists the "most perfect phonetic writing system in the world."

On a lighter side, it was missionaries from the United States who first introduced the apple (for which Korea is now famous) and the ubiquitous poplar trees that fit so well into the rural landscape of Korea that they seem to be indigenous.

It is difficult to measure the impact of Christian religious concepts and the other ideas that Western missionaries brought with them, ideas related to such things as individual freedom, human rights, equality of women, democratic politics, the rule of law, and certain matters of ethics and morality (relative to condemning the taking of bribes or maintaining mistresses or concubines, for instance). Certainly, the Koreans have been very responsive to the messages that inhere in or are connected with Christianity, as the rapid growth of numbers testifies.

4

Korean Values—Then and Now

Let's start by reviewing some basics about values. Our values are transferred to us by parents and others from the day we are born. They come from the words spoken to us and the behaviors we observe as well as from the role models we pattern ourselves after and those we discount. Values become embedded in our minds and, after our early years, lie out of our awareness, affecting in basic ways how we think and what we do. They are buried so deep and have such a strong influence that we often assume our values are universal and natural to the entire human species—and *right* as well. They also constitute a central element in our identity or how we conceive of and define our "self."

In examining, contrasting, and comparing specific core values, in this case those of Americans and Koreans, there are a few things we should take into account.

One is that in the United States, the identification of core values is clouded by the fact that we live in a multicultural society that has "melted down" people from numerous cultural backgrounds to produce a mainstream American culture. The U.S. is therefore a polyglot of cultures,* many of

---

* In sharp contrast, Korea is one of the world's most homogeneous cultures.

45

which are melting only slowly, if at all, and which deviate anywhere from a little to a great deal from the mainstream U.S. culture. Nevertheless, that mainstream American culture is the common currency of the society, so members of the microcultures, if they are to retain the specialness of their own cultural background, are forced to become bicultural if they want to communicate with people in the mainstream culture or in other microcultures within the country. Thus the identification of mainstream core American values in this kind of context is a valid and useful exercise for all Americans, regardless of their ethnic background.

Another important factor is that in isolating and examining specific values and behaviors of a particular culture group, we come up against the danger of stereotyping. While stereotyping is a natural psychological process that enables us to absorb, process, and usefully categorize the immense quantity of sensory data with which we are constantly bombarded, it can lead to false generalizations and judgments when we confuse our stereotypes with the individuals we are dealing with face-to-face.

Thus it is important to not allow the comparisons, contrasts, and generalizations we make regarding values and behaviors to lead us to stereotype either Americans or Koreans. While most of the Americans and Koreans you meet will reflect many or most of the values and behaviors described in this chapter, other individuals may deviate significantly. Nevertheless, it is valid, indeed necessary, to examine shared cultural characteristics if we expect to interact successfully in our cross-cultural encounters. Crossing cultures requires, over time, the comprehension of where each of the cultures is coming from and how it conceptualizes the world.

Before looking at the values themselves, it should be noted that Korean values have undergone a major shift within the last forty years. The change has been as radical as the value change that occurred in the Western world during the Industrial Revolution. The beginning of this change can even, in the case of Korea, be more or less pinned down to the years 1960 to 1965, but the changes continue in the lives of con-temporary Koreans to the present day—and beyond. I will begin my discussion of values by focusing on traditional pre-1960 Korean values as they compare and contrast with Ameri-can values, and then by examining the value changes that began occurring in Korea between 1960 and 1965 and some of the implications of these changes. American values have also significantly evolved and began changing in the latter half of the twentieth century, especially since World War II, but the change has not been nearly as dramatic or as contra-dictory as it has been in Korea.

In order to understand the enormous value changes that began to occur in Korea between the years of 1960 and 1965, it is necessary to realize that Korea, which had earned its identity as the Hermit Kingdom, was, in 1945 at the end of World War II, suddenly released from about six hundred years of domination by China. Added to this was thirty-five years of having been completely subsumed, forcefully and against its will, into the Japanese Empire, whose aim it was to destroy the last vestiges of Korean culture and convert the entire population into loyal Japanese citizens as quickly as they could. There were few nations in the world that were less aware of what was going on in the rest of the world than Korea in 1945. Since the early fifteenth century, Koreans had by their own choice become thoroughly Confucianized and sealed off from outside influences, and it was into this highly traditional culture that the American "liberators" suddenly arrived. Not only were they different physically, but the cultural values they brought with them were also way off the Koreans' values map.

No wonder it would take from fifteen to twenty years (from 1945 to 1960 or 1965) for the materialistic American culture to begin to penetrate a society that had always looked to the distant past, not to the puzzling and uncertain future, for its models. In addition to the sudden presence of large numbers of Americans, with their seemingly limitless resources to import everything they needed or fancied, hundreds and thousands of young Korean students could now aspire to travel to the United States, further facilitating the rapid shift in values to ones more closely resembling those of the U.S. That any of the original Korean values remain at all is the real miracle. Among young adults (between the ages of twenty-eight and thirty-five), few of the traditional values do remain intact.

Most of these changes in Korean culture began to have enormous materialistic implications, whereas the traditional values that survived maintained their heavy societal and humanistic grip on society.

As might be expected in any society experiencing such a drastic infusion of foreign values in such a short time, present-day Korea is a country with a wide generation gap, with many of the older generation as well as the dwindling rural population trying desperately to hold on to the older, more familiar values, while the younger generations have grown up and become more comfortable with the radical, new, heavily Westernized values. Yet the situation is not as clear-cut as this. What has been extremely interesting to me, in my role of cultural analyst, as I have watched Korea gradually grow to become the eleventh largest economy in the world (prior to the economic decline of 1997–1998), is just how much of the old, traditional value system still lies buried only skin-deep in even the most Americanized young Koreans I have known, especially among those whom I have encountered here in the United States. This is my rationale for going into considerable detail in explaining the old as well as the new ways, and why I have given so much attention (as, for example, in Appendix C) to the explanation of the customs and traditions as they used to be, as well as the changes that have and are continuing to come about. Not only are these changes interesting for the sociological background they provide, but in fact, the foreigner who interacts with Koreans today, whether in South Korea or in the U.S., must learn to do a quick, on-the-spot analysis of each person to determine just how traditionally Korean or how Westernized he or she really is. Even after you are confident that you have "figured them out," most Koreans will begin to surprise you with the tell-tale signs of a residual traditional Korean value still firmly in place.

It is also necessary for me to warn the quintessential American that the American values that you bring to the task are neither better nor worse than their counterpart traditional Korean values—only different. And, further, the ideal way to function in Korea is as a person who is sensitive to and interacts not only within a Korean or an American value system, but, as someone who is yourself in the process of becoming bicultural, able to successfully bridge both worlds and function in *both* value systems (consciously knowing when each system is appropriate for the situation).

Traditional Korean Values (pre-1960)

Now let's turn to a consideration of how the values of Americans and Koreans compare and contrast on the Kohls Values Continuum.† We will begin our examination with the two sets in sharpest contrast, as they appeared prior to 1960.

---

† The continuum and the discussion of American values that follow were adapted in part from L. Robert Kohls, *The Values Americans Live By* (Washington, DC: Meridian House International, 1984).

Figure 1: **The Kohls Values Continuum**

Traditional Korean Values (Prior to 1960)	Mainstream American Values
Acceptance of Fate	Control over the Environment
Stability, Continuity, Tradition	Change and Progress, "Development"
Priority: Human Relationships, Harmony	Priority: Time and Its Control
Rank, Status, Hierarchy	Egalitarianism, Fair Play
Group Orientation	Individualism, Independence, Privacy
Birthright Inheritance	Self-Help, Improvement
Cooperation	Competition
Past Orientation	Future Orientation
"Being" Orientation	"Doing" Orientation, Achievement
Formality, Protocol, Ritual	Informality, Innovation
Indirectness and Saving Face	Directness and Openness
Philosophical Consideration	Practical Application
Spirituality	Materialism

You will notice immediately that in these thirteen critical value continua, American and pre-1960 Korean value orientations are at opposite ends of the spectrum.

Americans often have difficulty talking about or, indeed, recognizing that they have values identifiable as American. They consider themselves, above all, to be unique individuals, not realizing that their belief in individualism itself is one of the strongest, most pervasive values they live by, and that in most of the cultures of the world individualism is not only a lesser value but, as in traditional Korea, is considered an undesirable one.

Americans also tend to deny the influence of external forces—family, friends, church, school, the media—in shaping who they are. They are much more comfortable believing they have personally chosen who they have decided to become, and many simply reject the idea that they share a "culture" with other Americans at all. A foreign anthropologist observing Americans could, nevertheless, easily produce a list of common values (similar yet perhaps varying somewhat from the list above) that would fit *most* Americans and would stand in sharp contrast with the values commonly held by the people of many other countries and cultures.

Let's look at the values listed on the Kohls Values Continuum one by one. The most important values will also be discussed in depth in later chapters.

1. Acceptance of Fate versus Control over the Environment

Belief in the power of fate is deeply rooted in the Korean psyche, derived from the Buddhist concept of karma, and it influences the thought and behavior of Koreans whether they are followers of Buddhism or not. While from an American point of view, acceptance of one's karma, or fate, results in a pervasive dead-end fatalism, it also fosters patience and an unhurried approach to life (since one can work out one's fate over any number of lifetimes), peace in the face of death, an explanation for evil, and acceptance of misfortune and adversity.

Clearly, much of the contentment and harmony that is so important to Koreans is supported by the kind of freedom from stress a belief in fate can foster. This contrasts sharply with the American disdain of fatalism; to be called "fatalistic" is one of the worst criticisms in the American value lexicon. From the American perspective, individuals from cultures who trust in fate are seen as superstitious, probably lazy, unassertive, and, in general, unwilling to take the responsibility and the initiative to bring about improvements in their lives.

Americans consider it normal and right that humans should take control of their own destiny. The problems of one's life are not seen as resulting from fate but as having come from one's failure at problem solving and self-improvement and as evidence of a failure to take responsibility. One of the most striking contrasts in this regard is between the "take-charge" American and the more passive, let-things-take-their-course Korean.

I have consciously chosen "Acceptance of Fate versus Control over the Environment" to begin our comparison of the two cultures because in a very real sense, whether or not one believes there is something larger than ourselves that controls what happens to us, this contrast shapes all of the other values on the Values Continuum chart. The American-European belief that *I* am in charge of *my own* life explains how and why Western cultures are so different from Asian (and all of the other more "traditional") cultures. Actually, the taking over of that control (beginning in the seventeenth century in Europe) is what marks the beginning of the modern world. We will see this difference play out frequently in subsequent chapters.

2. Stability, Continuity, and Tradition versus Change and Progress, "Development"

Korean society has evolved over a period of several millennia, so it is hardly surprising that tradition and continuity are highly valued and change is looked upon with suspicion, even fear. It is also not surprising that the value shifts that began to occur between 1960 and 1965 have resulted, in the present day, in a generation gap and substantial, even radical, changes in the society of the once Hermit Kingdom.

In the American mind, change is uncontestably good, for it is linked to development, improvement, progress, and growth. The conviction that we can do anything we set our minds to and that change is inherently good—together with a belief in the virtue of hard work—have resulted in striking social, economic, and technological accomplishments in the United States.

3. Human Relationships and Harmony versus Time and Its Control

As we shall see in examining Korean behavior in the chapters which follow, especially in chapter 6, Koreans place paramount importance on human interaction. In business and other economic affairs, smooth relationships are more important than efficiency or accuracy. Time constraints and schedules are not allowed to interfere with the pursuit of interpersonal relationships, which are critical to the establishment of trust and the ability to work together comfortably and harmoniously.

For Americans, efficient time management—getting the job done—is more important than "wasting" the time it takes to develop relationships and trust. This enables them to achieve, a prime American value, and to be productive. In the American view, not using time to some clear, practical end is a waste of precious resources.

The language Americans use with reference to time gives a clear indication of how much it is valued. Time is something to be "on," to be "kept," "filled," "saved," "used," "spent," "lost," "gained," "planned," "given," "made the most of," even "killed." As a result, schedules take on great importance, to the degree that they may rule one's life to the detriment of interpersonal relationships.

Koreans are surprised when in the United States to find that one has to make an appointment to see a friend, just as I was personally surprised to discover that the Korean language uses the same word (which translates into English as "to play") to describe two dignified, elderly gentlemen sitting on a park bench visiting with each other *and* young children romping together in the street.

4. Rank, Status, and Hierarchy versus Egalitarianism and Fair Play

Herein lies a major divergence between Korean and American values, one that will be difficult, even painful, for Americans to deal with when encountering the Korean culture.

Koreans by and large recognize and accept that human beings are unequal, and they have organized their society on that basis. This follows the Buddhist belief that it is right for one to have one's present place in society based on one's accumulated karma. It also follows the Confucian preference for hierarchy, ritual, and formality in the governance of human interactions, as well as the strong Korean orientation to ingroups and outgroups (described in chapter 8). One need not be concerned with those who are not part of one's clearly delineated ingroup.

For Americans, of course, the idea that all human beings are created equal is a most cherished belief (see chapter 5 for a fuller discussion of American egalitarianism). Also inherent in or complementary to egalitarianism is the unique Anglo-American concept of fair play. This idea transcends the particulars of group identity and of rank, status, and hierarchy, taking the form of an abstraction applicable in any situation no matter who the other person is, what group he or she belongs to, or what his or her rank or status is. The concept of fair play is not even translatable, at least not precisely, into most of the other languages of the world, and certainly not into any of the Asian languages.

Another subtle variation in the two cultures can be seen in how the words of our heading are defined in the two cultures. In the United States, there is a significant distinction between the two words *rank* and *status*: rank refers more to a person's job title, and status describes how one's worth is regarded by others. In Korea, the two blend together much more comfortably, because one is respected for bearing the title itself.

5. Group Orientation versus Individualism, Independence, and Privacy

Over the years, as I have worked in programs designed to orient East Asians to life in the United States, one of the first things I ask them upon their arrival in the U.S. is, "What is the smallest separable unit in any society?" From literally thousands of Koreans, Chinese, Japanese, and Taiwanese, I have heard no other answer than "the family." Then I tell them that, strange as it may sound, when I have asked the same question of American audiences, I have never received any other answer than "the individual."

Later, in recounting this interesting difference to American audiences, I tell them that if I were to respond to the Asian audience with "Oh, no, you don't understand, the smallest meaningful unit of society is not the group but the individual," it would be as unbelievable as if I were to respond to the American with "Oh, no, it's not the individual person but one of the billions of cells that make up your body that is the smallest meaningful unit." The typical Korean would find it as difficult to believe that an individual would try to operate on his or her own as an American would consider that a single cell isolated from the body would or could operate independently. One result of this strong Korean group orientation is the remarkable (to Americans) level of dependence on parents in what we judge to be a mature Asian adult. It is more common for Americans to blame their mother for the alleged damage she has done to the proper development of their character.

The individualism that has developed in the Western world from the Renaissance onward takes its most exaggerated form in the United States. Here, individuals are seen as separate and special, "endowed by their creator with certain inalienable rights." Americans are, first and foremost, *independent*; and while they do join groups, their loyalty is fluid. They don't see themselves as giving up their individuality or independence for the security that comes with group loyalty. A spin-off of individualism, of course, is the concept of privacy. Americans value their privacy to the point that when exposed to the constant presence of others in a group-oriented society like Korea, they tend to experience great stress and feel the strong need to spend some time alone. Privacy is viewed by Americans as giving them endless freedom. At the same time, Koreans, indeed all Asians, are far more likely to interpret the concept of privacy to be more synonymous with being alone and lonely, as if expelled from the group (and even by the larger society).

6. Birthright Inheritance versus Self-Help and Improvement

Simply put, birthright inheritance means having been born into the right family. As Americans (despite our media-driven fascination with a few very prominent families), we see being born into "the right family" as an "accident of birth" and reject its significance. To people who live in hierarchically structured societies, one's birthright is no accident, especially when, as in Korea, one couples the belief in karma and reincarnation with the strong feelings of superiority and worthiness that hierarchy and the concept of fate imply. Sociologists often refer to cultures that impute status through birthright as conferring "ascribed status" to those of "high birth"—in contrast with American culture, where status is "achieved."

The value Americans place on achievement translates into self-help. In the United States one only gets credit for what one does for oneself. In fact one even gains respect by having been born into a poor family and, by dint of hard work, having raised one's status in society on one's own. In Korea this would be next to impossible to accomplish. If the individual is autonomous, controls his or her environment, and believes in progress, then that individual has the ability, indeed, almost the obligation, to improve him- or herself, in other words, ultimately to "control one's own destiny," which is an utter impossibility if, by definition, destiny or fate is something that is outside one's control.

7. Cooperation versus Competition

The Korean group orientation (discussed in more depth in chapter 8) creates a strong ethos of cooperation with the people who are part of one's ingroup and a climate of fierce competition with those who are not—another company in the same industry, for instance. This cooperative orientation fosters an atmosphere of mutual support and concern for the feelings of others within one's ingroups, and at the level of family and close friends, a deep loyalty.

Americans are more inclined to compete with everyone, including those they are close to. They believe competition ultimately brings out the best in people or results in a better idea or a higher skill level. They encourage it in the home and at school in ways that startle and shock foreign visitors. Paradoxically, Americans also have the capacity to work together cooperatively on group projects with people virtually unknown to them—provided the cause is important enough, the goals specific, the tasks stimulating, and the project limited in its duration.

8. *Past Orientation versus Future Orientation*

Traditional Koreans look to the past in a Confucian context; that is, the past from which they seek their models is that of a mythical Golden Age of imagined perfection in which anything in the present or in an imagined future suffers by comparison. Americans, by contrast, tend to devalue the past ("History is bunk," said Henry Ford), and they barely take time to enjoy their present condition, which they think of as only a prelude to the future. They are enamored with the rewards they imagine the future to hold, which in any event cannot help but be better, and it is they—not fate—who will make it so.

9. *"Being" Orientation versus "Doing" Orientation and Achievement*

In a being-oriented culture like traditional Korea, one gains importance and respect not for what one has done, produced, or achieved, but for who one is, for one's quality of being. This is a common value preference in hierarchical societies, and whatever its shortcomings, it lends stability to the social structure. The being orientation gives credibility to class differences, calls for respect—even veneration—for age, and fosters a clear distinction between work and leisure.

Americans, of course, are intensely doing- or action-oriented. They like to keep busy, with a schedule of activities in which leisure is something one *does* as much as enjoys. They are defined by their work ("What do you do?" or "Where do you work?" is the single most common question Americans ask people they meet), and achievement is the surest determinant of status. This drive to achieve leads many Americans along the path to workaholism. One important value driven by the doing orientation (or perhaps vice versa), is the dignity of human labor (a leftover in some degree from the early immigrants, who rejected the European class system and left it behind). But the willingness of Americans of rank to engage in manual labor or physical work is, as we shall see, puzzling to people like traditional Koreans, who come from a more class-oriented society where a "gentleman" dares not have anyone see him perform even the simplest manual task.

10. Formality, Protocol, and Ritual versus Informality and Innovation

One would have difficulty finding a society where formality is prized more highly than in Korea. By contrast, mainstream American society is certainly one of the most informal in the world. Here, the two countries are at absolutely opposite poles.

In Korea, practically every relationship, except among immediate family members and the most intimate friends, is maintained with a level of formality Americans can hardly imagine. Given names are rarely used, and life is ritualized in almost every public situation. Americans call people by their given names immediately upon contact and practice and value informality in most aspects of their lives.

The formality that Americans encounter in Korea, however, no matter how often it rubs them wrong, gives them an advantage in their attempt to adapt. Rituals are easy to imitate (because one observes them being performed in exactly the same way, over and over), and the wise visitor will observe closely and follow suit.

11. Indirectness and Saving Face versus Directness and Openness

Indirectness and a concern for saving face—one's own and that of others—continues to be a paramount feature of all Asian cultures. It can still cause difficulty for Americans, who are known for their directness, even bluntness, and who too often respond carelessly and impatiently to the subtleties of indirect behavior. However, concern for the other person's face—the preservation of his or her sense of self-worth and personal dignity—is a substantive human emotion and should not be belittled or ignored. Americans, of course, value their directness and openness and are proud of their honesty and their insistence on "telling it like it is." In Korea, however, face-saving practices must be pursued because, as we shall see in the case study in chapter 6, the consequences of ignoring face can be disastrous.

12. Philosophical Consideration versus Practical Application

The Confucian ideal of the Gentleman Scholar who is averse to physical labor helps illuminate the value Koreans have traditionally placed on philosophical issues, abstract theory, and lofty thoughts—and which they prefer to more practical matters. Practical applications are, on the other hand, what Americans excel at and deem important. Indeed, they pride themselves in not being excessively abstract or theoretical. The American tends to run aground by believing that this practical, pragmatic way of thinking is universal, and begins rattling off the practical implications of some idea or the "logic" of his or her presentation. In Korea, one needs to give more attention to setting the stage and focusing on the theoretical foundations of one's subject. The rationale for taking a particular action will more likely be accepted if it can be connected with a practice in the past or to a Confucian principle.

13. Spirituality versus Materialism

Spirituality is used here in its broadest meaning, devoid of religious connotation and in clear opposition to the world of physical reality that surrounds us. In Korea it is related to the orientation toward the philosophical concerns and abstract theories described above. It also implies a lack of attachment, perhaps even an aversion to or an avoidance of, the world of real objects and the physical comforts one can derive from them. Instead of such comforts, the ideal Confucian Gentleman, as alive today as in the distant past, looks for intellectual stimulation and the adulation and respect he receives from a society that recognizes the worth of his "spiritual" contribution.

Americans, who are regularly accused of being acquisitive and materialistic, stand in sharp contrast with Koreans in this regard. From the Americans' perspective, material possessions are a sign that they have been diligent in their engagement in hard work and successful in their achievement of the goals they have set for themselves. In short, they feel they *deserve* the physical comforts and material objects they enjoy.

Korean Value Changes (post-1965)

These thirteen contrasts above, then, are the ways in which American values compare with those of pre-1960 traditional Korea. They inform cultural and behavioral patterns you will encounter frequently, especially in older Koreans. But, as we have already discussed, about 1960 to 1965 was when Korean values *began* to change, and there have been radical changes occurring since then. These changes come from many factors and forces at work in Korean society, not the least of which have been the traumatic effects of the economic crisis that came in late 1997 throughout East and Southeast Asia, resulting in the breaking of the "social contract" and the resulting unprecedented layoffs by the large conglomerates. However, the greatest erosion of the traditional Korean values I have described came with the "migration" of Korean students to the United States to pursue graduate degrees. It would be difficult to exaggerate the effect of the exposure to core American values, especially on Koreans in the twenty-five to thirty-five age range. The impact of experience in the U.S. and with thousands of Americans, beginning about 1950, has played a major role in driving the value changes that have resulted.

Yet among younger, more modern Koreans, the old values often still lie deep within, the new values constituting only a veneer. Even though they may appear to behave in ways and live in a style typical of Americans in any large city in the United States, they are still Korean at the core. Thus, in assessing the changes that have occurred in Korean values, keep in mind that it will often be difficult to tell where the Korean you meet is coming from; perhaps he or she is the product of a modern, industrialized society, but maybe much of that appearance is only on the surface (with the traditional values, shaken and damaged but still more or less intact, below), or possibly he or she appears very traditional but more modern values lie out of sight until some event brings them to the fore. When first-time Western visitors arrive in ultramodern Seoul, with its contemporary architecture, its familiar highway interchanges, its stock market, its abun-

---

‡ First came the "vedio bang," a place where young people could sit and watch movies at an inexpensive price. Some vedio bang owners soon turned their stores into "computer game bangs." Others added on-line trading features. Once what is now called "PC bangs" were known to make profits, those who lost their jobs during the 1997–1998 financial crisis began plowing their money into this business. The result is that thousands of PC bangs have sprung up.

dance of cell phones, and a computer bang‡ around every corner, they will think they are in familiar territory. Only time and the accumulation of their daily experiences will bring them to the realization that there *is* in fact a difference in the way most Koreans act. Ultimately, this implies a fundamental difference in the way they think as well. When you have arrived at this point in your own awareness, you will understand the title of this book.

Figure 2 identifies (with bold type) the general direction in which Korean values have shifted for many modern Koreans of today, certainly for those who have been responsible for causing the post-1965 "economic miracle."

Figure 2: Post-1965 South Korean Core Values (*shown in bold type*)

Acceptance of Fate	**Control over the Environment**
Stability, Continuity, Tradition	**Change and Progress, "Development"**
Priority: Human Relationships, Harmony	Priority: Time and Its Control
Rank, Status, Hierarchy	Egalitarianism, Fair Play
Group Orientation	Individualism, Independence, Privacy
Birthright Inheritance	**Self-Help, Improvement**
Cooperation	**Competition**
Past Orientation	**Future Orientation**
"Being" Orientation	**"Doing" Orientation, Achievement**
Formality, Protocol, Ritual	Informality, Innovation
Indirectness and Saving Face	Directness and Openness
Philosophical Consideration	**Practical Application**
Spirituality	**Materialism**

What I am attempting to illustrate in Figure 2 is the *direction* in which the value changes are moving, not necessarily the full effect of the changes, since they are still occurring. The boldface values in the left-hand column are those where Korean values have remained relatively static and are likely to remain constant for the foreseeable future.

One observation that is immediately apparent is the degree to which the changes have taken place in the value areas most likely to cause or at least facilitate the dramatic economic changes that began to occur in Korea between 1960 and 1965. In contrast, those values that have remained fairly constant seem more related to social and political matters, which may reflect the fact that political changes (toward greater freedom, for instance) have been much slower in coming to present-day South Korea but have become more obvious since the late 1980s.

It is also time to put this discussion of values in the context of the Korean "economic miracle," which the world has observed taking place in recent decades, as well as the economic crisis that followed in late 1997 and 1998. Although in this chapter we are crediting the dramatic shift in values as being responsible for the miracle, we hasten to point out that the values shift was only one of a number of factors that occurred in unison to bring South Korea into the modern world economically.

First we should note the reciprocal influence of value change and economic development on each other. The more the change in values has affected the course of economic development, the more economic and technological forces must have driven changes in values.

Another factor was the effort President Park Chung Hee (1963–1979) mounted in the initial years of his term in office (no matter that this was reversed later in his presidency) to stamp out the centuries-old patterns of bribery and corruption. This effort had, in turn, its own effect in shaking up some of the dysfunctional aspects of the old value system and setting the new in place, at least temporarily.

Also important was the fact that Japan, after its total defeat and extensive destruction in World War II, was successful in rebuilding its economy and becoming the first Asian country to prove itself equal to the West. This astonishing accomplishment provided both a stimulus to Korea's development and a model, which they followed to the letter, finding it exhilarating to begin competing with Japan, their former (1910–1945) hated "master."

There were other elements also: the fact that South Koreans, like the people of so many countries during their era of industrialization and rapid technological development, began their mass migration to urban areas, where the value changes largely took place; strong government support, protection, and funding for economic expansion (perhaps, in fact, too much government support or at least for too long a time); popular enthusiasm created by the stimulus to compete with Japan economically; and finally the cumulative effect of decades of being the recipient of millions of dollars in assistance from the United States as well as the silent influence of thousands of Americans who descended on Korea after World War II. All of these and many more factors were the ingredients of South Korea's rapid economic development.

For many Koreans today, those who have been or are in the process of becoming modernized or Westernized, the biggest change lies in their assuming full personal responsibility for what happens to them, rather than simply relying on fate to run their lives. By taking charge of their own life, they have been able to cause the change they desire to actually come about; they have seen it happen, and the observable effects have made them far more proactive than the typical Korean of the past. Yet still today, the self-made Korean who was not born into a high social position is not admired and respected to the degree of the one who was born into the upper class. Confucianism (which considers the world of business and commerce to be a rather undesirable profession) still dictates that the person who acquires wealth through buying and selling will not be admired, no matter how wealthy he or she has become, as much as the well-born man or woman.

In the shift from cooperation to competition, too, there is a noticeable difference between Koreans and Americans. In their shift to competition, Koreans retained their group orientation rather than becoming individualistic. That is, their emphasis remains on cooperating with those in their ingroups while simultaneously being highly competitive with their outgroups, that is, with other companies in the same line of work.

The task for the Westerner who is trying to figure out the similarities and differences between the U.S. and the Korean views of the world is considerably complicated. Just when you, the Westerner, think you have decided that Mr. Kim is definitely one of the modern Koreans, evidence of some of the more traditional Asian values will surface. Then, again, this is always the case when a traditional society begins to modernize. Value changes are never clear-cut, definitive, and decisive. Traditional values persist, at least with the older generations, while new, brash ones are being tried out. In fact as the old values are called into question, more Koreans fall back on the security provided by practicing the old values. What I am describing, then, is a process that is both dynamic and subtle. At present both conflicting values sets are still very much in evidence. Korea is a society in transition, if ever there was one. Furthermore, if you think all of this is bewildering to you, consider for a moment how utterly confusing it must be to the Koreans experiencing the turmoil of such drastic values change.

Korean Values at the Beginning of the Twenty-First Century

Korea is one of the most dynamic countries in Asia, whether measured by its rate or breadth of change. In the last five years South Korea has been hailed as an economic miracle, derided as a failed business model, applauded for the rapidity of its turnaround, and denigrated for its failure to reform. North Korea has been on the brink of invasion, on the brink of collapse, on the brink of nuclear conflict, and now suddenly might find itself on the brink of reunification. The Korean people have seen more changes in five years than many countries see in twenty-five.

Predicting what will happen next week in Korea is difficult enough; predicting the next century is an exercise in utter futility. However, one thing is certain. A number of trends among young people in Korea today are surely shaping the society of tomorrow, and that society will be unlike anything Korea has seen in the past.

The first major trend is the urbanization of the population. Nuclear families are now firmly established as the norm rather than the exception, as people move out of the country and into high-rise apartment blocks in the city. Certainly, families generally still live very close to each other, but today's teenagers are not growing up in households that they share with their grandparents. As the current baby-boomer generation grows older, it is likely that Korea will face difficulties in supporting an increasingly graying population. Currently, the demographic bulge in Korea is in the thirty- to forty-year-old age bracket. In twenty years, this group will be looking to retire, and their children are unlikely to take their aging parents into their own homes.

Young people are becoming much more independent. Whether this is because of the pervasive influence of Hollywood, the increased wealth among the middle class, the relaxed discipline that comes from living in a two-generation household, or a mixture of all or none of these, young Koreans today behave in a way that would have been unimaginable ten years ago. Some of the changes are small—the sudden diversity of hair colors, for example, or the exotic sense of fashion that would, literally, have led to arrest in 1990. (In 1995 two girls were arrested in the city of Kwangju and charged with public indecency for exposing their navels.

Today, one of Korea's most popular singers appears on stage in a halter top and a skirt cut so low over the hips that it seems in permanent danger of losing its battle with gravity.) Some of the changes are larger—increases in premarital sex and young people moving out of the family home to live alone. Some of the changes are huge—the massive increase in international travel and the widespread overnight approval in South Korea of North Korea's "Dear Leader," Kim Jong Il.

Young people in Korea today demand a higher degree of freedom and a better quality of life than any generation before them. The business of entertaining Korea's fickle youth has given rise to brand-new enterprise sectors overnight and destroyed them almost as quickly. In 1997 the BB-gun shooting gallery replaced the video arcade as the ultimate cash cow. That gave way to banks of photograph machines that would transfer your image onto a sticky label along with a range of graphic designs. That in turn surrendered to the DDR (Dance-Dance-Revolution) machine, a hip-hop lesson cum aerobics session cum video game. Predicting next year's trend correctly could make one a very wealthy person.

The Korean twenty-something generation behaves like a flock of birds on the wing. Everyone goes in the same direction for a while and then, suddenly and with no warning or discernible cause, the entire flock abruptly heads off in an entirely different direction. That trend is exacerbated by the staggering profusion of mobile communication devices and on-line services. In the mid-1990s the accessory of choice was the pager. Everyone had one, from grandparents to middle-school children. This was a cultural phenomenon of enormous impact. Suddenly, young people did not have to take personal calls on the family phone. Instead they could sit in plush coffee shops and exchange voice messages over their pagers. The trend gave rise to a whole lexicon of "pager chat." Young Korean men would page their girlfriends, leaving a contact number and the suffix 1004. One thousand and four is *chŏn-sa* in Korean (which is, coincidentally, also the word for "angel"). The suffix 82 (*bali*, pronounced "pal-ee") meant call back immediately (*bali* is the Korean word for "quickly").

The pager trend was relatively short-lived, though. The mobile telephone PCS (Personal Communications System) service exploded in Korea in the last quarter of the 1990s, replacing the pager and beginning the competition among Korean telecom companies. Today, almost 50 percent of Korean people have a cellular telephone. Thoughout its Confucian history, Korea has always been a highly networked society. The advent of the cellphone has brought young people together just at the time when the traditional networks are beginning to dissolve. The result is an environment in which ideas and trends flow very quickly among young people, largely liberated from parental oversight in a country more open to international influence than ever before.

As young people become more freethinking, they begin to reject the way of life that their parents followed. The traditional career path of school to university to company to retirement to grave is rapidly being eroded. Rigid management hierarchies in traditional companies are proving too restrictive for new employees. A demand for an improved quality of life is sending people out of the office at an earlier hour. Korea is even considering implementing a five-day workweek, an unthinkable innovation in the days of "Korea Inc." This change is slow to come, as the twenty-somethings are only now entering the workforce. However, the seeds of change are planted deep.

Perhaps the most visible sign that all is not as it was is the increasing number of women in the workplace. The role of women in the office in the past was to look pretty, make tea or coffee for the boss, and marry one of the office workers. At that point a woman's career was over. It was time to go home, cook, clean, and have children. Ironically, modern Korean women are at least as well educated as the men—often more so—and yet only recently has this role begun to change. The *chaebŏl* conglomerates remain bastions of conformity, where women play a largely subordinate role. However, more and more foreign companies are setting up shop in Korea and providing serious career options for Korean women. The increase in the service industry is also proving an area where women are coming into their own. In the public relations industry, for instance, women often outnumber men by as much as three to one—or more.

One thing is certain. If Korean marriages ever approach equality between wife and husband, it will be the younger generation that brings it about. Korean men, in general, are reluctant to give up the power and privileges their maleness has provided them for centuries.

Increased empowerment for women has its corollary in the gradual feminization of men. In traditional Korean society gender roles were very clearly defined—the man earned the money and the woman took care of the house. As more women develop independent careers, though, their husbands and partners are slowly playing a greater role in raising children and tending to house chores. Very few Korean men over the age of forty know how to cook even the most basic meal. Young Korean men with working wives are learning how to look after themselves—or losing a lot of weight. This trend, if it continues to develop, could well lead to reduced stress among Korean men as they devote more time to their families and their quality of life and less to late-night social drinking sessions with colleagues and business partners. (Stress-related illness is currently the number-one killer of Korean men.)

The closing of the gender gap is very much in its infancy, and its effects are not yet particularly widespread. It will be some years before the evidence of changing gender roles will be seen in society. However, the final trend to be considered—the Internet—has already had a massive impact on Korean society.

Korea is a nation of technophiles. Perhaps even more so than the Japanese, Koreans embrace new technologies with an enthusiasm that is staggering. The Internet revolution hit Korea like a freight train and has barely slowed down. Take a trip on the subway in Korea and try to spot an advertisement that is not for an Internet company. Seven of the top twenty most-visited Websites in the world, and thirteen of the top twenty Asian sites, are Korean. Korea has registered more Internet domain names than the United States and sees an additional three hundred Internet companies start up every day. By the end of 2002, an estimated 40 percent of Korean households will have broadband Internet access, and the volume of on-line business will be in the tens of billions of dollars.

The Internet provides yet another means to maintain the personal networks that are an essential part of Korean society. Korea's most popular site is a hotmail-style, free e-mail provider that has been in business for about five years. Number two is iloveschool.com, a newcomer less than one year old that provides a forum for people to contact their old elementary-, middle-, and high-school friends. The iloveschool.com Website is the fourth busiest site in the world in terms of page hits. The PC bangs provide cheap, high-speed Internet access for e-mail, Internet browsing, and on-line gamers and stock traders (Korea also has the world's highest rate of on-line stock trading). There are even successful businesses being run out of PC bangs.

The dot.com boom of 1999 saw a massive increase in the number of Internet-related businesses and a corresponding exodus of young professionals from the aforementioned restrictive, hierarchical chaebŏl into new, dynamic high-tech start-ups. The typical Korean Internet entrepreneur dresses like an investment banker and often holds an MBA from a prestigious international university. The brain drain from the chaebŏl is forcing businesses to rethink their working conditions and to provide greater incentives for people to take the corporate road over the information superhighway. As dot.coms become dot.bombs, many of these young entrepreneurs are choosing to stay independent rather than go back into the chaeböl. At the same time, the number of high-profile bankruptcies and near bankruptcies among Korea's traditional corporate flagships has shaken many people's faith in the lifetime security of a corporate career.

By 2002, the Korean government is determined to have a commercial, third-generation mobile telephony network in place. Korean people will be able to browse the Internet; download audio and video content; and use video-phone technology, global positioning, and a whole host of other services, all from a mobile handset. To what extent will this innovation spur further social liberalization in Korea?

What impact will the opening of North Korea have on today's twenty-somethings? How far will increasing democratization and the opportunity for increasing personal freedom affect their personal and professional decisions? How will they adjust to Korea's expanding role on the international stage—and the corresponding presence of international businesses and organizations in Korea? How long will it be before Korea can put the turmoil of the Asian currency crisis behind it and fill its potential role in the global economy?§ Every development seems to open the door to a hundred more questions, and the answers are changing almost hourly.

It is almost as though Korea is going through a developmental stage similar to the late 1960s in Europe and the United States, an age of increasing freedom and decreasing certainty, of New Age euphoria seasoned with the fundamental questions about what the purpose of life really is. Where will the country be twenty years—or even five years—from now? Few people would be rash enough to make a prediction. One thing, though, is certain: Korea will make fools of a great many analysts for a long time to come.

---

§ Just prior to the 1997 economic crisis, the *Economist* magazine had predicted that South Korea would move from its rank as the eleventh largest economy in the world to the seventh largest by the year 2020.

5

Barriers to Thinking Korean

Here we will discuss a few of the many attitudes and beliefs that make it difficult for Americans to adapt to living in Korea or, in what I believe is the fitting title of this book, *Learning to Think Korean.*

The first barrier is the fear that adapting to another country's cultural patterns will somehow make you less American. All you need to do is think of studying a foreign language to see how impossible that is. When you study French, you do not become French, no matter how fluently you learn to speak the language; and, more importantly, you do not forget how to speak English!

Learning another culture—or learning to think in another culture's way—is like learning another language, an *additive* process, and you can add as many new languages and new cultures to your repertoire as you have the time and energy to master. Becoming adept at understanding the customs and ways of another culture does not intrude on your enculturation as an American. That process has been going on for far too long to be affected by a few years of cross-cultural input. What learning to function appropriately in another cultural setting does—in addition to enriching you as a human being, a value of no small significance—is simply make you feel more at home and able to function more comfortably and effectively within that culture.

The second barrier is Americans' strong desire or need to believe that, deep down, all people are the same. I call this the "Magoo cop-out." Mr. Magoo, the myopic movie cartoon character, was able to misunderstand, misinterpret, or simply miss everything going on in the world around him because of his assumption that everything in the world conformed to the mistaken preconceptions his vision was powerless to correct. He could travel to Albania or Algeria or Afghanistan and never realize that he had left the comfortable shores of his own country. People after all, his sightless instincts told him, were the same everywhere. Many of us are so like Magoo. This inclination derives from a relatively complex psychological process, but the result is that Americans often have major difficulty in accepting the differences they encounter in others and in adapting to the fundamentally different values and patterns of thinking and behaving they find in other countries and cultures—an idea that is dangerously close to "closed-mindedness."

The third barrier is the particularly virulent strain of chauvinism with which many Americans are infected. We have from early on been a boastful lot—things American are simply, without question, the biggest and the best. Since about 1950 our boasts have gained credence. By the turn of the twenty-first century, the United States had some of the world's most advanced technologies, one of the highest standards of living, and the most powerful military; we had developed the first nuclear bomb, put the first man on the moon, and consistently produced the highest annual gross domestic product in the world. More than that, there has been no country that has had the ability to act as a magnet to the world's immigrants the way the U.S. did and still does. While this might help one understand why Americans so easily succumb to a belief in their natural superiority, the problem is that when you leave the U.S., you learn rather quickly that

this homegrown patriotism looks to everyone else like jingo-
ism or false pride.

The fourth barrier to being successful in learning to think
Korean is those same value contrasts we explained in chapter
4. Some of these values reflect basic assumptions about the
way the world works. These assumptions in their totality are
unique to each culture, and Americans are as thoroughly
indoctrinated with these assumptions as are the members of
any other society.

The problem lies in the fact that we are never told they are
merely assumptions. Indeed they have been put into our
heads as though they were *not* assumptions at all, but external
truths, and they lie so deep in our psyche that we never
question them. We simply assume that any intelligent, right-
thinking person would agree with us that they are "Truth"
with a capital *T*. In other words we come to believe, eventually, that these "truths" must be universal in their acceptance
by human beings, that they are an inherent part of human
nature. They are not. They are *cultural*. Let's look at an
example of one of these deep-seated assumptions, the American concept of equality.

Equality, from which we derive our cherished values of
egalitarianism and fair play, is enshrined in our political
documents, and we have given it a religious basis by stating
that "we are all equal in the sight of God." People are created
equal, according to the Declaration of Independence, though
physical, intellectual, and behavioral evidence might lead us
to experience otherwise. Although we translate the idea economically and socially into "equality of opportunity" and
politically into "one person, one vote," and although the
society is replete with examples of people being treated un-
equally—for instance, in our persistent racism—the assumption that human beings are and/or should be equal and should
be treated equally is buried deep in the American psyche and
is rarely questioned, even in the face of its blatant violation
by those who believe it so strongly.

Since seven-eighths of the people on the planet think otherwise, Americans can be considered almost unique in this belief in equality. Most of the rest of the world assumes that people are not created equal and values rank, status, and authority instead. Rank, status, and respect for authority give people a sense of security and certainty that Americans are rarely likely to feel. It can be very reassuring to know, from birth, who you are and where you fit into the complex system we call society. There is something rewarding—even if you are at the bottom of the heap—in realizing that the services you render, the role you play, and the place you have are indispensable to that society.

The fifth barrier is the most difficult one to address because it is buried deepest of all. It deals with the ways in which we structure our thoughts and the thought process itself. It is necessary for us to come to grips with it, however, if we are ever to learn to think Korean. The difficulty lies in the fact that our brains have already been programmed to structure our thoughts in the American way, just as the brains of Koreans have, in their way. And the thought patterns and cognitive styles that are dominant in Korean culture are radically different from those that predominate among Americans. This barrier probably will not strike you until you actually move to Korea (or another non-Western culture) and attempt to apply Western logic—on the assumption that it is universal. It is a profound experience to discover that "alien" mindsets govern the most basic processes of thought and logic in other people. See chapter 9 for a discussion of the futility of Western logic in the face of requests for favors.

Here are some of the most significant ways in which Korean and American patterns of thinking diverge.

Differences in Patterns of Thinking

1. Concrete versus Projective Thinking

The Korean mind, programmed to deal systematically with

the concrete, is much better prepared to respond to the separable mix of microevents which occur in any given macroevent than the American mind. Americans tend to be so busy trying to understand how the elements interrelate that they are less likely than Koreans to take careful, detailed notice of all of the individual components.

Americans will ask, for instance, "What does it mean?" and "Where does it lead?" Americans have been programmed by their culture to engage in a form of analysis which orients them as quickly as possible and enables them to predict likely outcomes, that is, to project into the future in order to head off mishaps.

Koreans are more content to notice what is, without being bound by a mental scenario which demands that they understand the relationship among the elements and project its meaning into predicting the future.

2. Associative versus Cause-and-Effect Thinking

By "associative thinking," I mean that Koreans tend to be aware of all of the separate individual people and separate elements that are involved in any given event, and to associate them together vis-à-vis that event, but never ask which among them *caused* the event to occur. Until the large-scale intrusion of Americans into Korea (1945 to the present), Koreans were unfamiliar with cause-and-effect thinking, which plays such a dominant role in the Western mind that it is almost impossible for an American to conceive of anyone thinking differently. Yet the basic thought patterns of most non-Western cultures are such that unless specifically trained in Western logic, their people simply cannot conceptualize this (to us) "natural" way of observing the world. It is not hard to learn. It only requires that one be made aware of a strict, single-track series of sequential minievents, where the first event is credited with having caused the second event, which, in turn, causes the third, and so on ad infinitum. Westerners become so good at predicting and interpreting the path of cause and effect that we can come in at midcourse and read the situation backward as well as forward.

Koreans, like most non-Westerners, unless they have been specifically trained to think in this way, are far more likely to simply accept what is without trying to discern what caused it to become that way.

3. Deductive versus Inductive Logic

Americans have a preference for reasoning inductively—which relates to the preference for projective thinking. They gather discrete facts and, by sorting and analyzing them, come up with general principles. Koreans, like the French, prefer deductive logic in which they begin with the general principles and then adduce examples that illustrate or follow from them. This difference in approach has a pronounced effect in the application of training techniques (see chapter 12) where Koreans prefer to be informed by an authority, while Americans like to participate in a process of discovery (managed by an authority—the "trainer" or "facilitator"— who is acting as though he or she were their equal).

4. Inconclusive versus Conclusive Orientation

Americans and Westerners in general tend to believe that anything inconclusive or open-ended is unfinished and thus wrong. They therefore like to bring things to a conclusion, to finalize them so that they know where they stand. Koreans, like other East Asians, are much more comfortable with open-endedness, with leaving things vague and unstated. This manner works to their advantage in negotiations (see chapter 10), where Americans, driving toward completion and trying to nail everything down in reaching an agreement, find they have given up too much in meeting their need to conclude matters.

As with our discussion of traditional and acquired Korean values in chapter 4, the discussion of how traditional Koreans think versus American thought processes focuses on both sets seen as polar extremes. I must here repeat my warning that you will find present-day Koreans falling into every possible slot between the two extremes, with younger Koreans having been heavily influenced by American and Western European mindsets, especially if they have studied abroad. Part of the fun of interacting with young, modern Koreans lies in trying to determine what particular mix of values and thinking processes predominates in each person.

Korea: People-Oriented and Group-Centered

The next four chapters will make you aware of what you need to know about Koreans, ideally before you meet them. More than one American has commented on initial aspects of Korean culture that they found troubling. Michael Breen, in his book *The Koreans: Who They Are, What They Want, and Where Their Future Lies*, says it this way: "The Koreans have a way of upsetting you and getting into your heart at the same time." For me personally, that happened so long ago that I remember only the good parts, but I continue to run into Westerners who are more mindful of the things about Korea and Koreans that have turned them off.

Yet, many Westerners I know who know the Koreans, the Chinese, and the Japanese equally well end up being particularly charmed by the Koreans, claiming it is easier to work your way more deeply into the Korean culture than into either of the other two.

I have also discovered that Koreans, in spite of their reluctance to show their emotions openly (which I describe elsewhere in this book), seem to have an almost immediate reaction to each individual Westerner, and if they like you, you know it, and if they don't, you can sense the nonverbal signals pretty quickly too. I suspect these responses have something to do with sincerity (as discussed below) and are triggered by the Koreans' reaction to its presence or absence.

Korea is a people-oriented society. In the United States we are more fact-, cause-, or progress-oriented, more fascinated with machines and technology than with people. We are also more interested in pursuing and achieving a preestablished goal, in attaining the most profitable bottom line, or in being sure we use our time productively (as noted in chapter 4, page 53). There is nothing wrong with these values, but as we become busier and busier, we find we have less and less time left to spend with our families and friends. And the less time we have, the more we are likely to maintain friendships by relying on a most impersonal machine—the telephone (or, increasingly, e-mail)—to keep in touch with one another. All of these American characteristics, plus our emphasis on seeking our own advantage over all others, tend to make us more "selfish" as we pursue our own interests.

Sincerity

One dimension of this people orientation is embodied in the Confucian concept of sincerity (*sung shil*, see chapter 3). True sincerity may be as rare in Korea as it is in the United States, but it is far more highly valued there. In each culture sincerity fosters trust between individuals and leads to the growth of a deep and lasting relationship. This becomes even more of a concern in Korea; I have long believed that Koreans seem to have been endowed with a sixth sense that enables them to unerringly detect insincerity wherever it exists. For many Americans sincerity is often applied *insincerely*, as in many of our advertisements about companies that "care about you" or in our behavior at, say, cocktail parties where we meet new people. In such settings Americans often act as though they are interested in their new acquaintances, but they are actually using the occasion to promote themselves and to make a good impression.

In the Korean interpretation of sincerity, people who bad-mouth their own country or the company they work for are said to be insincere. Someone who must, for whatever reason, refuse to do something a friend requests is thought to be insincere. If someone who claimed to be your friend and who had enough money to do whatever you, as a friend, requested, yet chose not to do it, that person would be judged insincere by most Koreans (more on the implications of this perception of friendship is found in chapter 2, Critical Incident 6). Also considered insincere would be the person who publicly claims to have accomplished certain professional goals before actually having done so. Koreans also think that anyone who goes around constantly smiling at everyone they see (as Americans have been socialized to do) is, by Korean definition, insincere. As you can see, the ways in which sincerity and insincerity are defined are quite different in the two cultures, and there are likely to be misunderstandings over precisely what they mean.

Even more fraught with the danger of misunderstanding is the concept of face. Face is intimately connected with how we relate to other people, and Koreans attach great importance to maintaining in themselves and others a full sense of respect, which allows them to retain face at all costs. When a person has committed a wrong, Koreans ask whether it is a bigger sin to have committed the wrong or to openly humiliate the person who has done so.

Face

Nothing seems, at first encounter, to puzzle the American who tries to understand Korean culture more than does the matter of face. Nor can an American conceive of the almost sacred role face plays in maintaining a Korean's sense of dignity and status in society. It is in this respect that face must be included in even the simplest introduction to Koreans as a people-oriented society, for it is in preserving face—

the other person's as well as your own—that an absolutely sacrosanct respect for people is most clearly being demonstrated. In effect, it is in the preservation of the human dignity and self-worth of that person, even when truth itself must be violated to preserve them, that the fundamental worth of the person is being demonstrated to be of utmost importance.

Here is a case study that will help to illustrate the complexity and the high priority given to face in Korean culture. It is followed by a discussion of the subject which will throw light on the issues that arise in the incident.

The Case of Kim, the Copyboy

I have just had a remarkable experience. My head is still spinning, not so much from the incident (which was bad enough) but from the "explanation" of it by Mr. Lee, whom I respect and who has worked with Americans for more than fifteen years here in Seoul. That's what's incredible—Mr. Lee's explanation. He's actually blaming me for Kim's wrongdoing.

Kim is a copyboy and general errand runner for an English-language newspaper where I am employed as the only American on the staff. I came to Korea after getting tired of the jobs I'd had after graduating from college (where I did a combined major of English and Asian studies, which isn't as unusual as it seems). My job here is to put into acceptable prose and polish the copy that has been translated by one of three translators from Korean into raw English. I know little Korean myself, so I can't check the accuracy of the material in the original. I also have to rely on the three translators to interpret anything I must communicate to my co-workers. Not speaking the language is frustrating, but the English rewrites keep me so busy that there's little free time for me to communicate with anyone anyway.

I'm trying to learn Korean, but it's a slow and discouraging task. Every time I attempt to use a new phrase, my co-workers laugh at my pronunciation rather than responding in a normal way to my just-memorized question.

That's why I try out what little Korean I have learned on Kim. He, at least, has taken me seriously. He has also asked me to help him with his high school English lessons. I have felt rather sorry for him. He couldn't be making much money in his job as a flunky, and his clothes are rather worn-out. Since he has to work his way through school, he's forced to go to an inferior night school rather than one of the better day schools. Yet I've never seen anyone more diligent. Whenever there's a moment between errands, Kim is studying. Because everyone else is above him, he is ordered around as if he were dirt. Even with the little Korean I've mastered, I can tell they're talking to him in the most disrespectful, even contemptuous, language.

Before today, I've felt sorry for him and have never spoken roughly to him or ordered him to do anything. In fact, I've befriended him whenever I've had the chance and helped him practice his English. I've appreciated having another person around with whom I can communicate at least a little in English. Until today, I felt I was helping him and that he deserved it. A couple of times I've bought his lunch when I was sure he wasn't eating simply because he couldn't afford to. He never thanked me, but I just supposed he was ashamed to be so poor. But let me describe what happened, and you tell me whose fault you think it was.

Kim had been hanging around my desk for most of the last hour of work. I would look up every now and then and exchange a sentence or two in English. I had to continue working, but I wanted to be sociable too. The interruptions were good for me, so long as I didn't overdo them, and I was the one who was "setting the pace."

When it came time to go, Kim made no move to leave. Instead, he just talked on. I had put my work away and finally said, "Well, it's time to quit and go home." But instead of leaving, he accompanied me down the stairs and out of the building, walking a half step behind me.

On the sidewalk the thought struck me that maybe he was hungry and in need of a meal. Since I had nothing planned for the evening, I decided to invite him home for dinner. It took no urging on my part, as it sometimes does with Koreans. He was noticeably pleased and accepted right away. His step livened, and he began walking beside me rather than behind, as he had been doing. Also his English suddenly seemed more fluent. It wasn't really any better, but he spoke with more confidence. It was almost as if he hoped his school buddies would see him carrying on a conversation with his American friend as we walked together to my home. Although I didn't think of it at the time, I'm sure he had to miss his evening class in order to accept my invitation.

By American standards, my small apartment isn't much. I live in two sparsely furnished rooms, with a small compact-disk player, an old electric typewriter, a color TV, and some borrowed furniture. There's not much more. One wall is covered with books, paperbacks bought new or from secondhand bookstalls, which are surprisingly well supplied with English-language titles. They overflow the bookcase, actually. No one throws books away in Korea.

You should have seen his surprise when he entered my apartment. He was clearly impressed. His eyes took in everything. They moved from item to item, but they kept returning to the books. He probably had never seen so many in anyone's private collection before. "Like a library at university!" he said. I'm sure he thought I had shipped them from the States, because he was astonished when I told him I had bought them in Korea. "They're no big deal. A lot of them are used. Someone else owned them before I did." I tried to downplay what apparently seemed to him great wealth. He could never dare hope to own such an extensive personal library. For a moment I considered giving the whole collection to him when I leave Korea.

As I started to cook dinner in my tiny kitchen, I tried to continue our conversation. It was difficult because I needed to concentrate on my task, while he needed every gesture I could give to illuminate my statements.

I finally gave up and suggested he choose a disk from the pile and play it. He started shuffling through the disks, but it soon became apparent he didn't recognize any of the pieces or enough of the English to make an intelligent selection. He eventually chose one and inserted it in the player. It was Handel's *Messiah*, and it was nowhere near Christmas.

Then the incident occurred. I happened to glance up to say something at the very moment that Kim picked up my gold Cross ballpoint pen and slipped it into his pants pocket. I saw him take it, and he knew I'd seen him, but he didn't seem to be the least bit chagrined at being caught. He acted as if nothing had happened. He didn't offer to put it back, though he could not have had the slightest doubt that I knew what he had done.

I really got angry. I was showing him every kindness, in the office and now here at home, and this was how he repaid me. What kind of fool did he think I was? He might be able to steal from me behind my back, but when he saw that I observed him do it, he should at least have had the decency to admit his error and put my pen back.

I can't remember exactly what I said, but I exploded. He may not have understood my rapid-fire English, but he could hardly have failed to get my point. I was simply not going to let him get away with it. If he'd never learned right from wrong, I would teach him. After a minute or two he finally began to act a little ashamed, so I let up, assuming he would put the pen back and apologize (enabling me to apologize for blowing up). Instead, he suddenly dashed out of the apartment. I felt a little bad that I'd been so hard on him and that he had left that way, before we had eaten, but mostly I was indignant at what he had done.

When I got to work the next morning, I went to see Mr. Lee, an editor at the newspaper and a friendly man who had advised me on occasion about things Korean. I told him what Kim had done and asked his help in straightening Kim out and in getting back my pen, which had been a special gift to me from a personal friend and had a great deal of sentimental value.

You can imagine my shock when Mr. Lee took Kim's side against me! His reprimands were gentle, but it was clear he disapproved of what I had done. In fact, he was incredulous, not that Kim had stolen from me but that I had called him on it and right to his face. Mr. Lee questioned me pointedly: "You invited him into your home? You treated him as an equal? You were preparing dinner for him with your own hands?" He was clearly implying that I had been to blame!

What surprised me most, however, was when he said, "You left your pen out where he would be tempted?" Surely it wasn't wrong to leave my pen lying on the table in my own house.

Then Mr. Lee came to the real point, and his speech became slower, calmer, more deliberate. It was as if he suddenly realized that he had to explain the most basic aspects of human etiquette to this uncivilized foreigner. And to do so would take all the Confucian grace he could muster (though I didn't fully understand this until much later). "Let's go down to the tearoom for a cup of tea," he said.

I looked at my watch and, a bit densely I realize now, said, " I don't know if I've got time. I've got an article to get out before eleven o'clock."

"Never mind. That can wait. Let's go down for tea, and I'll explain to you."

He didn't say anything on the way down, and I didn't either. After ordering tea, he pushed his chair back from the table and stared off into the distance. "Kim won't come back to the office," he said.

"What do you mean, he won't come back to the office?"

"You've made him lose face, and there's no way he can ever work with you now."

"I've made *him* lose face?" I said, raising my voice, incredulous now in my turn. "*He* is the thief!" Mr. Lee seemed embarrassed by how loud and angry I was, but he was obviously determined to go through with his explanation, painful though it was.

"Yes, that was wrong on his part. Stealing is always wrong. But what you have done, I am ashamed to say, is far worse." His voice dropped so low I could hardly hear it. And what I did hear I couldn't believe. Kim had stolen from me and it was my fault! But I was too confused to be angry. How could Mr. Lee explain something so illogical? He stopped a moment and then changed course. "How much did your pen cost?"

"It was a gift, but it probably sold for forty or fifty dollars, plus tax, several years ago."

"Don't you think Mr. Kim's human dignity is worth more than forty dollars?" he asked. His words were without malace, though he was obviously determined to straighten out my warped set of values. "And the worst part of the situation," he went on, "is that once it's done, there's no way, ever, to undo it."

"Oh, yes, there is," I said. "All he has to do is say he's sorry and ask my forgiveness."

Mr. Lee hesitated for a moment, until he realized that I had completely misunderstood him. "No, you don't understand. I didn't mean there's no way to correct the wrong he committed. I mean there's no way to undo the wrong you have done. Once you've made a person lose face, there's no way to say 'I'm sorry. I shouldn't have done it; let's be friends again.' Loss of face is forever. The only thing the person who has lost face can do is remove himself permanently from the presence of the person who caused his shame. In some cases losing face can cause a person to commit suicide."

"Even if I forgive him and ask his forgiveness?" (though I still wasn't ready to do that).

"Yes, even if you did that, it wouldn't do any good," Mr. Lee said simply.

We spent the next few minutes in silence. Finally Mr. Lee said, "People are more important than pens," answering his own earlier question. "And much more delicate also."

I'm still stunned by Mr. Lee's comments. I hope he has exaggerated the gravity of the situation in order to underscore his point, but somehow I sense he hasn't. I haven't thought of anything else all day. It's as if what I've always known as white is suddenly black, as if up is down. It's going to take some long, hard thinking to work my way through this one.

I have a terrible feeling, though, that Mr. Lee is right; I'll never see Kim again to tell him I'm sorry for what I did and to ask his forgiveness.

Discussion of Face and Comments on the Case of Kim, the Copyboy

The concept of face is tied closely to the notions of shame and guilt. Koreans, and other Asians, come from "shame cultures," where behavior is governed more by a wrongful act's *being made public* and the culprit exposed for doing wrong than by his or her having committed the act itself. There is no loss of face simply because someone sees you do wrong. That's true even if you know that someone saw you do it, so long as that person does not *act* on that knowledge by exposing your wrongdoing. (This is one of the major points being made in the case study.)

In a guilt culture, one develops (or is supposed to develop) an "internal police officer," a conscience that keeps one from doing wrong. This stems significantly, of course, from the Judeo-Christian religious tradition. In a guilt culture, then, you experience guilt whether anyone else finds out or not. "After all," Americans say, "you have to live with yourself." In a shame culture, you only experience shame if and when you are *exposed*.

Americans and other Westerners lose face also, but far less easily than East Asians do, and it is not the major determinant of behavior that it is in Asian cultures. And as an American, if you find you have done something—either intentionally or unintentionally—to embarrass someone, you can make amends fairly easily. You apologize—and if you embarrassed someone in front of others, you must apologize in front of those others as well. That won't work in Korea. As we have seen in the case study, the biggest sin is not the stealing (though stealing is considered wrong), it is the humiliation and loss of face of another person. Or as Mr. Lee says pointedly, "People are more important than pens."

Loss of face is the most serious matter a Korean can imagine, and once face has been lost, there is no way ever to restore it. The American in the case study is stunned when he realizes that Mr. Lee is angry about the wrong the American has done in causing Kim to lose face. "Loss of face is forever." The only thing the person who has lost face can do is remove himself permanently from the presence of the person who caused his shame.

Most Americans would almost certainly feel that a person who has done some obvious wrong and shows no remorse, as Kim did, should be taught a lesson by at least being publicly humiliated and forced to make amends—if not be put in jail. But the loss of face for the thief would, from the Korean point of view, be the greater evil, done by the person cruel enough to *call the thief* on what he had done; that is, to make an issue out of it.

Most day-to-day matters of face will not lie at such extremes as in our illustrative case study, but the importance of face in Korea must never be discounted or treated with arrogance. Americans will have to work hard to understand this kind of feeling for others, using all the imagination, empathy, and forgiveness they can muster.

Simply put, in a face-conscious culture, Westerners need to be constantly concerned not to cause another person to be embarrassed or humiliated, or to lose face. This involves not saying anything critical of another person to his or her face, especially not in the presence of someone else and, in general, not doing anything that would make that person look bad or threaten his or her rank or reputation. Similarly, you should avoid acting in a way that would embarrass you, your family, your company, or your country.

It does not require a great deal of imagination to see that, given this background, it would be a difficult task, for example, for a Korean to write a frank performance evaluation of an employee under his or her supervision (as he is asked to do in chapter 2 in Critical Incident 7).

Kibun

In view of the foregoing discussion on face, it should not be surprising to find that Koreans are highly conscious of their general state of being and that of those around them, especially when things are not quite right. It is a gut feeling— similar to the sixth sense they have about sincerity—that tells them something is troubling you, even if, when they inquire, you are not aware of it yourself.

English vocabulary gets cumbersome trying to describe this sort of feeling, but Koreans have a precise word for it—*kibun*. *Kibun* means the state or condition of a person's inner feelings, the mood one is in, how one feels about oneself, and the strength of one's sense of self-worth. It is of utmost importance to Koreans and to their immediate interaction with another person that they both be at their happiest and best. That, too, is part of what is meant when we say that the Koreans have a people-centered society.

Clearly, then, Koreans are not going to do anything that would disturb the other person's kibun. This means not informing someone, especially if he or she is a foreigner or someone of high rank and authority, about unpleasant things that may have occurred. It means that when something must be said, telling white lies to make the occurrence seem less catastrophic or traumatic in order to soften the blow is the best solution. Whatever needs to be done to keep from upsetting a person's kibun, or positive sense of self-worth, must be done. If one continually points out unpleasant aspects of a situation, he or she is an unpleasant person to be around, and Koreans will soon begin to avoid that person in order to safeguard their own kibun.

Indirectness and Harmony

It is not hard to identify the pitfalls awaiting Americans who subscribe to the rugged individualist's creed of being straightforward and direct, "telling it like it is," "letting the chips fall where they may," and "calling a spade a spade." In the United States, such a truthful and direct person can serve the valuable function of getting us back on track when we've strayed from reality. It doesn't work that way in Korea, where it is considered rude to make comments that challenge or refute what the other person has just said. Such a restriction means, of course, that it is extremely difficult—virtually impossible, in fact—to carry on what Americans would call a true discussion. Even the slightest deviation from the other person's perspective must be made by the subtlest hint rather than boldly or argumentatively. This is an art requiring such skill that, as Westerners, you and I may never hope to master it fully, yet the attempt to do so is beneficial and can even be pleasurable in itself. In Western countries, though more strongly in Europe than in the U.S., everyone is expected to have a different idea from everyone else. It is seen as part of what makes each of us unique, and we are expected to express our own individual opinions, to explain them if necessary, and to defend them against disagreement. In Korea, it is considered more important to avoid saying anything that might offend or disturb the harmony of those involved in the interaction and to always defer to the person of highest rank or status.

If one is expected to protect the harmony of those one is involved with, it stands to reason that saying no to someone should be avoided at all costs. This is one aspect of Korean culture that is extremely difficult for Americans to adapt to. To Americans a "simple yes or no" is the easiest, clearest, most certain of all answers. In Korea a foreigner will rarely even hear no, so yes becomes the problem. A Korean yes does not mean "Yes, I agree with what you have just said, and yes, I will do it." It merely means "I have heard what you have said, and now I will go ahead and do whatever I wish." Or perhaps it means "I really prefer to say no, but since it would be impolite to do so, I will say yes but mean no."

Saying no is impolite, so Koreans do anything to avoid it, especially to a foreigner, even if it entails saying yes while meaning no. John Condon and Mitsuko Saito once wrote an article entitled "Sixteen Ways to Avoid Saying 'No' in Japan."* In Korea the number of possible variations is about the same.

When they need to say no but cannot, Koreans are likely to become suddenly vague and appear very uncomfortable to have been put in such an embarrassing position. They may say something like "It is very difficult" or "It's not convenient right now" or "I think there are others who may be better able to do it than I" or "I'll try to do it" or "I'm not sure if I will be able to do it." Or they may offer the excuse of how busy they are at the moment or that they are not feeling well or have a prior obligation—anything to avoid using the word no. Older Koreans may simply say nothing but suck in a long, noisy breath of air through their teeth to indicate how difficult it will be. But more likely, they will simply say yes and mean no.

Similarly, one should also be warned that Koreans rarely respond with "I don't know" to a question asked them di-

---

* In *Intercultural Encounters with Japan: Communication—Contact and Conflict* (Tokyo: Simul Press, 1976).

rectly. Such a blunt confession would cause an embarrassing degree of loss of face. They much prefer giving a made-up-on-the-spot answer rather than none, so one can never be confident that an answer is correct. The wise foreigner will ask several Koreans (and perhaps a few foreigners as well) the same question and will compare the answers given. Indeed, the pursuit of the correct answer to a single question can keep you busy for at least a few years—if you decide to take on the task as an enjoyable one. (It is, I assure you, the most pleasurable game foreigners living in Korea can play.) I'm sure you have guessed by now that Koreans will not expect their foreign boss or co-worker to admit to not knowing the answers to their questions.

In keeping with their penchant for indirectness and the maintenance of harmony, Koreans are not likely to look you directly in the eye, particularly if they are trying to show respect or deference. If you catch them doing so, they will usually quickly avert their glance, and it most likely means they are taking a *nunchi*, "eye measurement." This is done surreptitiously to gauge your response to the interaction with a view to modifying what they are saying so as not to communicate something with which you seem to be in disagreement or find offensive. This is an indication of how important they consider it to be to maintain harmony at all times. In the Korean language, the verb comes at the end of the sentence, which gives Koreans more flexibility than English speakers have in altering what they are saying in midsentence.

This sparing but specific use of eye contact underlines the importance of kibun, of protecting or maintaining what is sensed of the mood and feeling of the other person in order to preserve his or her kibun, self-respect, harmony, and in the extreme, face.

A corollary to this hypersensitivity to disharmony or causing discomfort to the other person by inappropriate eye contact is the Korean's ability to simply not see someone unexpectedly caught in less than complimentary circumstances—

such as catching the boss with his tie askew and his feet on his desk or coming upon a man relaxing in his underwear on a public train. The interloper looks quickly away until out of the range of sight or until the other person is properly attired and self-possessed, after which both parties act as though neither noticed anything wrong.

But, you might ask, how (or when) does one who is always concerned with maintaining harmony and avoiding discomfort express his or her emotions? The answer: Never! It is more complicated than that, of course, but the answer for you, nevertheless, is Don't! Ever! at least, not in public.

Direct, public expression of one's emotions is considered by Koreans a sign of immaturity and a sure indication that such a person is not someone you would want to be involved with. Yes, you will see people who, in the midst of the unbearably hot and humid dog days of summer, lose their temper when someone runs into their car, and who then cut loose with a stream of invective you can comprehend quite well even if you can't understand a word of Korean. But you do not want to be thought of as being such a common person yourself, so the advice is still Don't! Ever!

If a reprimand bearing some emotional content must be given, let an intermediary do it at a later, more appropriate moment, far out of the range of your delicate foreign ears. Messages of a corrective nature may also be transmitted through hints and subtle references, so subtle that they would go right over the average American's head. To drive the point home, the key phrase (still in all its subtleness) is repeated softly over and over again, almost as if musing to oneself.

Naturally, any society that has developed as many rules on how to behave as Korea has could be expected to have some officially sanctioned ways of releasing pent-up emotions. There are several. One of the most obvious is drinking. Koreans let off steam by getting drunk. But take care; never lay a hand on someone who is drunk. No matter how obnoxious and abusive a drunken person gets (and it is usually men), he is not considered responsible for his actions or capable of defending himself, and anyone who attacks him will be roundly condemned. Office workers often eat and drink together in Korea as a means of developing team spirit, and drinking is valued as a means of release from the tensions that have built up during the day, as it is in Japan. Another means of release lies in the readiness of Koreans to unload their true feelings on their closest friend, which probably saves a great deal of money—money which, in Western societies, might be spent on psychiatrists.

Collectivist versus Individualist Societies

All of the cultural characteristics of Koreans we have explored in this chapter are typical of collectivist cultures: sincerity, maintaining one's own and others' face, kibun, harmony, and indirectness.

Asian societies have always been group-oriented. As such, they share many characteristics with the seven-eighths of the people of the world who are also collectivistic. They are taught from birth to subordinate their individual interests to those of the group. They learn that maintenance of harmony within the group is considered of utmost importance, and any sign of chaos or potential discontentment within the group must be eliminated as quickly as possible. Those who hold power and status within the group tend to be revered and their actions never questioned or their positions threatened. The group's elders are respected and their wisdom valued. On a daily basis, they are more likely to interact with the same limited group of their own people—most of whom they have known from birth—all their lives.

Extreme ethnocentrism, the belief that their own group is innately superior to all others, is held as the common view, and all others are viewed as outsiders and therefore suspect and not to be trusted. Change tends to be seen as destructive, while traditions are valued and institutionalized. One's position within the society tends to be determined by birth into the "right" families rather than by one's cumulative achievements. Formality, protocol, and ritual are valued over creativity and originality; hence, the pressure to conform to established ways is strong. Those who break society's rules are often punished severely. It is generally difficult for outsiders to be taken into group membership. These are only a few of the many ways in which the more collectivist societies of the world resemble each other.

In a graduate class I taught recently,[†] we brainstormed more than two hundred and fifty characteristics which are applicable to most collectivist groups around the world (see below). The eight categories into which they fell are listed below with a typical example from each. It is significant that fifty years ago each of these statements fit Korea perfectly. Equally significant is the fact that while they still fit some Koreans, they don't fit those who may be moving in the direction of individualism. Above all, the changes are always subtle and occur at different rates. And as the changes intensify, Koreans increasingly fall back on the security of the older values.

Returning now to the theme of the characteristics of collectivist cultures, here are the eight broad categories and an example of each.

1. Family: The family (rather than the individual) is seen as the smallest indivisible unit in society.

2. Workplace: Those in leadership positions tend to hire their relatives and friends over strangers, regardless of qualifications.

3. Group Orientation: Subordination of individual interests and desires to those of the group is mandatory.

[†] At the Center for the Pacific Rim, University of San Francisco. I am indebted to Lauren Mallas for collecting the mountain of contributions and combining them into eight categories.

4. Status: A person's place in society is usually ascribed by "birthright" rather than based on one's record of accomplishments.

5. Conflict Avoidance/Maintenance of Harmony: Members are reluctant to argue with someone who has expressed an opinion the members disagree with.

6. Beliefs: Acceptance of fate is common.

7. Past and "Being" Orientation: Pride in the family's or clan's past achievements is common, and then becomes a model for the future.

8. Economic Considerations: Relative poverty is likely to be seen as the norm and accepted as inevitable.

In all of these ways, Koreans (and all Asians) have always had collectivist cultures. The situation will change in many ways (and a majority of Korea's citizens have already begun this transformation, as we have indicated above and in chapter 4), but whether Korea will ever cease being a collectivistic culture and become fully individualistic remains to be seen. I have my doubts. All we can say with certainty is that the value changes already occurring are carrying it in that direction, but then it is also true that the values it has held constant are the very ones that argue for it to remain people-oriented and collectivist. (Refer again to Figure 2 on page 62.)

Status and Behavior

Status

From the Korean point of view there is no such thing as equality among people. Even identical twins are born at least a few seconds apart, and age gives the older one seniority. Consequently, all relationships are between what Koreans term superiors and inferiors (or seniors and juniors), with that hierarchy defining one's status in each relationship.

In the United States, where equality is an ideal, we nevertheless would be forced to admit, if we gave it any serious thought, that no two people are ever precisely equal. We have simply agreed to ignore our differences in status and act *as though* we are equal, since we prize equality so much. Koreans, on the other hand, have agreed to recognize and admit that any two people are always unequal and to develop their relationships on the basis of that inequality.

Confucius identified five proper relationships in society: subject to king; son to father; younger brother to elder brother; wife to husband; and friend to friend. It is easy for the average American to see how Koreans might agree that the first three relationships could be considered unequal ones, but we are likely to think that the wife-to-husband and friend-to-friend relationships surely must be based on equality of feelings and behavior. Yet in Korea the husband still holds a higher status than his wife, and the friend who is older, though by only a little, ranks precisely that much higher in the friend relationship than his or her companion, and the two of them must never forget it.

Given this status consciousness, the possibility of upward movement within the traditional hierarchy is quite limited, and the hierarchy established in the Chosŏn (or Yi) Dynasty (1392–1910), which is still somewhat intact today, looks roughly like this:

Figure 1: Traditional Confucian Class Structure

	Royalty	
High	Landed Gentry, Scholars High Officials, Bureaucrats Clerks, Record Keepers	*Yangban* Status
Middle	Farmers, Craftsmen, Artisans Merchants, Businessmen Military Personnel	
Low	Outcasts: *Kisaeng* (similar to geisha), Entertainers, Beggars, Prostitutes, Criminals, Butchers	

As we look at this ranking, several things stand out. In Confucian Korea the landed gentry and the Gentlemen Scholars stood at the top of the social ladder, right below royalty (Confucius' first proper relationship). Given their obligations to the state, they were also the source of government officials and high-level bureaucrats, winning for these positions a degree of respect virtually unknown in the United States. To a surprising extent, this attitude persists to the present day. Corrupt officials have taken their toll on their profession's reputation, but Koreans tend to devalue the particular bureaucrat (once that person's dishonest acts have been exposed) while at the same time presuming the worthiness of the profession as a whole. In the U.S. people tend to sneer at bureaucrats as a group, even though most are honest and hardworking.

In the five hundred years since the class structure of the Chosŏn Dynasty was established, changes have naturally occurred, though fewer than one might suspect.

Figure 2: Modern Class Structure

High	Professors, Bureaucrats, Landlords, Upper Class (through family inheritance), Business Executives, Judges, Lawyers, Medical Doctors, Famous Television Personalities, Movie Stars
Middle	Teachers, Business Managers, Artists, Blue-Collar Workers, Military Officers, Farmers
Low	Construction Workers, Day Laborers, Beggars, Prostitutes, the Handicapped, Criminals

Professors, bureaucrats, landlords, those who are independently wealthy (especially if they have inherited the bulk of their money), and those who have been born into the "right" families are still respected in Korea to an extent that the typical American finds difficult to comprehend.

In Korean history these upper-class members have made up the yangban, the most respected members of Korean society (see Figure 1). Traditionally, merchants, businessmen, and military personnel were considered very low, even below farmers. Today, however, most successful business executives are included in the upper classes, along with new categories such as lawyers, judges, professors, and medical doctors. Indeed, despite the rigidity of the Korean social structure, social mobility is increasing, though one's place in Korean society is still much more likely to be set by one's father's occupation and position (i.e., whether one comes from a respected family) than it is in American society.

Older people are respected, regardless of their accomplishments or status (Confucius' second and third proper relationships). In the old days, for instance, this meant that one would not smoke or drink in front of an elder, and certainly one would not disagree with anything an elder said. In the family, this deference is even stronger; elders are honored, pampered, and appeased and therefore wield a great deal of power.

Again, for Americans, this takes some getting used to—whether you are on the giving or receiving end. Given the youth orientation of American society and the struggle many people endure to maintain their youthfulness as they advance in age, the first time a Korean calls an older American "Grandfather" or "Grandmother" is guaranteed to have a traumatic effect on the person so named. But rest assured, it is the highest compliment a Korean can possibly bestow on anyone.

Koreans coming to the United States are inevitably shocked to see so many older Americans living alone or, worse yet, in old people's homes. It would be difficult for a Korean to conceive of a worse fate. One of the most difficult questions you will be asked is "Why do Americans treat their old people in this cruel way?" The answer, of course, is extremely complex and cannot be dispatched with a twenty-second reply. But in the end, even the fullest and most thoughtful explanation will not satisfy; it is simply incomprehensible to a Korean. Incomprehensible or not, however, Koreans are headed in the same direction. Already many older Koreans who, in their earlier years, took care of their own aging parents, can no longer expect their own children to take care of them after they retire.

The question of how to deal with the aged is universal in human society. It was solved in traditional Korea by mandating that the eldest son inherit not only all of the wealth of the family, but also the obligation to take in and care for his aging parents. This age-old social security system, however, is breaking down as young Koreans are increasingly following Western social models.

Another indication of how differently Koreans view growing old is the *hwangap*, a special ritual which celebrates the fact that an individual has completed the sixty-year cycle (of the expected life span) and is now ready to move beyond the harsh rules and obligations of his or her earlier years and enjoy the rest of life free of restrictions. It is a particularly satisfying time for older Korean women, upon whom society had placed more limits and heavier burdens in their younger years. (See Appendix B for an explanation of the sixty-year cycle of the zodiac.)

A look at the Korean language reveals another aspect of the status of age. It is impossible to say *brother* in Korean without specifying (by using a completely different word, not just an adjective denoting older or younger) either *elder brother* (*hyung*) or *younger brother* (*dongseng*). More important by, strictly speaking, it is impossible to speak to another human being in Korean without either speaking up or down to the person, depending on your status compared with the other's. That difference, and there are multiple levels of it, is normally carried in the verb ending, which adds to the difficulty in learning the language for Westerners. There are also many instances when you use an entirely different word when speaking of yourself doing a particular act (eating, for instance) from the word used when someone else is doing the same thing.

A second group to whom rank- and status-conscious Koreans still show the utmost respect is their superiors. These include any and all superiors. Americans, who are much more inclined to question authority than to defer to it, notice this behavior especially in the workplace, where Koreans seem excessively deferential and submissive to their bosses and supervisors.

Korean management is authoritative and hierarchical, a top-down system in which relationships are based on differences in rank and the display of proper acknowledgment of that disparity. The employer-employee relationship will be discussed at length in chapter 11.

There are also other determiners of status. One of them is being born into the "right" family, such as having inherited land (see Figure 2). In the United States one's class or status is usually based on one's economic or professional accomplishments. In Korea wealth is not as paramount a marker of success. Like almost all Asians, or at least all Asians who have been born into the right families, Koreans are much more class-conscious than the typical American is, and those Koreans who have been born into the right families look down on those for whom being nouveaux riches is their only claim to fame. The most respected Koreans have family registers which may go back 1,200 years or more. This kind of ranking is like being a part of the nobility in Europe. These registers are, however, taken somewhat less seriously than they were a quarter of a century ago.

One of the most important status indicators in Korea is found in the answer to the question "What school did you graduate from?" which quickly sorts out the graduates of Seoul National University (considered Korea's top school) from all the rest. This question is as appropriate for the elementary school graduate as it is for a Ph.D.

Because of the central role scholarship and teaching hold in the Confucian social system, teachers have an inordinately high status among Koreans. Students' reverence for their teachers lasts a lifetime and has a major impact on their lives. This is partly due to the great value Koreans place on education but is combined with the general deference Koreans give to their elders. It also reinforces the tendency for students to be docile in class and discourages the kind of independent inquiry Americans value in their educational experience.

One of the most difficult relationships for Americans to adjust to in Korea is that of master and servant. Korean servants are unequivocally inferior to their employers, and it is embarrassing to the servants and offensive to Koreans of higher rank to treat them in any way as equal, to introduce servants, for instance, to your higher-ranking guests. It has been eighty years since servants were common in American middle-class households. The mere idea of servants is foreign to us, which, combined with our egalitarian impulses, makes it hard for us to order them to do something instead of asking them if they would please do it. If you speak Korean, the imperative to surmount your egalitarianism is reinforced because the language demands that you talk down to servants as inferiors.

In chapter 6 the case study involving an American of considerable status and Kim, a high school student who acts as a general errand boy, touches on status as well as face. Mr. Lee was incredulous when he found that the American had treated Kim as an equal: "You invited him into your home? You treated him as an equal? You were preparing dinner for him with your own hands?" The Koreans in the office thought it strange that the American would want to have a relationship with someone from the lower class.

To recapitulate, in Korea one's status is determined by (1) the family into which one has been born, (2) one's level of education and which university one graduated from, (3) one's age and one's title and seniority at work, and (4) to a lesser (but increasing) degree, one's current financial situation.

The Status of Women

Gender inequality will be very apparent to the sensitive, politically correct American living in Korea, and it will not help to be told that Korean women, in the old days, were said to have it better than their counterparts in most other Asian countries. Nor is it likely to lighten one's concern to know that Korean women really "rule the roost" behind the scenes in their own homes. The fact is that the double standard is at least as firmly in place in Korea as in any other society, and Korea certainly still qualifies to be called "a man's world."

Perhaps it is not even an exaggeration to claim that Korea heads the list of countries where women, as a class, are devalued. Domestic violence in Korea is said to be among the worst in the world. The women's movement, although heard of, has made relatively little progress there. What changes in gender inequality that have occurred are most evident in the business world, but even there, progress is painfully slow. There are no female CEOs of major Korean companies. Those few who have made it into the ranks of management report the same sorts of sexual harassment (made all the more difficult because there are no laws against it in Korea) and the same glass ceiling as women in the United States have experienced. If the corporate world has been slow to bring women into management positions, the government has been even slower. In the bureaucracy, fewer than 1 percent of the upper positions are occupied by women, and those are largely in the social welfare arena. Women professors are in the minority on university faculties and are definitely not treated as equals by most of their male colleagues.

We have already made the point that Korea is more influenced by Confucianism than any society in the world, and one of the basic tenets of Confucianism is that women should be subordinate to men and should defer to them at all times, even allowing them to claim credit for things their women counterparts have accomplished. Many Korean women, especially those born prior to 1960, seem resigned to being secondary to their husbands. And to justify this difference in treatment, one often hears repeated the Chinese saying "When a girl is young, she is ruled by her father; when she marries, by her husband; and when she is widowed, by her eldest son."

However, if Americans, both men and women but espe-cially those women who go as spouses accompanying their husbands, can come to terms with this aspect of Korean culture, they will find Korea a delightful place to explore. And Korean society affords foreign women a higher-than-usual status, which can ease the cross-cultural challenges somewhat.

Korean women now have equal standing with men under the Korean Constitution regarding equal pay for equal work and equal inheritance rights. Yet the majority opinion, still, among men and even among many Korean women, does not support this legal equality, and most often the equal benefits fail to materialize. In fact many Koreans view the women's rights movement as a Western idea that is being imposed upon Korea. It is seen as cultural imperialism and as such is resented and openly resisted. This opinion is not held by Koreans alone. In fact, the women's rights movement is much stronger in other Asian countries, such as Malaysia, Singapore, and China.

While educated Korean women are aware of the changes brought about elsewhere by the women's movement, it brought little to Korean women and is unlikely to do so in the immediate future. In fact, the situation has, if anything, changed for the worse as public opinion has hardened against having their traditional Asian values disparaged and allow-ing the United States, in particular, with its insistence on the universal application of human rights, to dictate Western values to them.

You will recall in our discussion of Confucianism in chap-ter 3 that one of the five relationships Confucius suggested as models that could define how people should relate to each other was the relationship of wife to husband. To Confucius, this was a fully unequal relationship, with the wife consid-ered to be in the inferior role to her husband. He was to be her master, and she was to obey his every command.*

A Chinese saying, one that most Koreans would agree with wholeheartedly, is that raising a daughter to marry into another family is like fattening a hog for someone else's banquet. Sons, on the other hand, were (and still are) prized because they did the heavy farmwork when Korea was 80 percent agricultural, rather than the 10 percent or less it is today, and carried on the family name in a culture where kinship was (and is) of utmost importance and where that relationship is passed on through the male lineage. Sons also cared for their parents in their old age.

In spite of this subordinate role automatically assigned to women, those who have been familiar with Asian cultures have long held that women's status has been less onerous in Korea than elsewhere, certainly when compared with Japan, or in pre-Maoist times in China. It is also often pointed out that it is the wife, not the husband, who has her way in all of the major decisions affecting the raising of the children. Much of the above assertion is in the category of what we might call "old wives' tales," but then, in this case, it is the old wives themselves who are defending the relative freedom they claim to possess.

It is the Confucian-based customs that are linked to the manner in which one's marriage mates are selected that will ultimately change the subordinate role of women in Korea, and it is the current generation and the succeeding ones who are and will be the ones to eventually break that hold. It is this tradition that Korean young people have already chal-

---

* The best single source on the extent of Confucian influence on the treatment of women in Korea is Martina Deuchler's *Confucian Transformation of Korea: A Study of Society and Ideology* (Cambridge, MA: Harvard University, 1992). For a direct translation of the relevant original Confucian documents, see Peter H. Lee's *Sources of Korean Tradition*, 1996, vol. 1, 458–63, 471–75, 491, 495, 496, 500–10, 558–74, 603, 604, 613–20.

lenged the most. At least among middle- and upper-class Koreans, girls now receive good educations, and parents are concerned that their daughters marry into good families.

In the past, and up to perhaps three decades ago, one's marriage partner was likely to have been selected by one's parents and elders in the kinship clan, who assigned the primary responsibility for finding the proper spouse to a marriage broker, as go-between. The broker carefully matched the wife-to-be and husband-to-be based on the social standing of their parents as well as the agreement of both families and the horoscopes of both candidates. Until about fifty years ago the two principals would likely not have even laid eyes on each other until the wedding day. That custom has been slowly eroding over the past half-century, but more often than not, marriages are still a compromise agreement. Currently, the parents of the couple may still do the choosing, then introduce them and give them a chance to go out together once or twice, and then give the couple at least veto power in the final choice.

If, as is increasingly the case, the young man and woman meet at the university or in their workplace, fall in love, and decide (on their own) to marry, they are still likely to seek their parents' blessings on the union. Also, the pressure Korean parents put on their daughters and their sons (as they reach marriageable age) to get married is still immense. When a twenty-seven- or twenty-eight-year-old Korean son has not yet married, he can expect that pressure to be exerted in most of the conversation that occurs between him and his parents. In the old days, a Korean male, regardless of how old he became, was not considered an adult by official standards until he married, and a woman was not respected until, having married, she bore her first male heir.

Of course, the education of well-to-do Korean daughters at universities—which are now often coeducational institutions—both in Korea and, especially, in the United States when they have been sent there to pursue graduate degrees, is also having its effect on changing the way Korean women are being treated, and especially on how their lives can be expected to change in the not-too-distant future. But those changes have not yet become as drastically modified in Korea as they have in Japan, for example, where the revolution is already well under way. One cannot help but notice, though, that divorce is far more common in today's Korea than it was twenty years ago. Another practice that is becoming a common occurrence is for the husband's mother to keep the couple's baby during the week so that both the husband and wife can work.

Older Korean women, provided they have long since married and produced at least one male heir, are, after they have reached the age of sixty and celebrated their hwangap, given more-or-less full release from the strict rules of feminine etiquette they have lived by up to that time. They have faithfully followed all of the rules, and now they are given freedom to do pretty much as they please.

To date, the most obvious change in the way that all but the most conservative men have come to treat women is their response to foreign women. It is often through their international business contacts—most likely through meeting the wife of an American or European business partner—that they have first met a foreign woman and realize that she cannot be forced into the invisible role to which Korean women have become accustomed. Even when first introduced, as she accompanies her husband, smiles pleasantly, looks them directly in the eye, and offers them her hand in a firm handshake, they realize that they are dealing with a very different, and even defiantly independent, woman, someone who is every bit her husband's equal in the conversation that she is emboldened to initiate. And they realize they are dealing with someone who will not allow herself to be pushed into the female role as it has been hitherto defined in Confucian Korea.

For the American expatriate woman who is deeply into the

women's movement, the role of Korean women may not be acceptable. One thing is certain, however: to the extent that she demands the right to "pull out all the stops" in bringing the full message of equality to Korean women, both she and her husband will fail on their Korean assignment. There is a valuable lesson to be learned here. Koreans have learned through more than six hundred years of being governed by overly aggressive foreign rulers, whether they were Mongols or Manchus or Japanese warlords, that the best way to defuse the overly aggressive alien masters is to never allow yourself to be anywhere they are likely to be; that is, to avoid them completely. And when you cannot avoid them, always agree with them politely, even thank them for "teaching you how to operate in the proper way," and then go ahead and do whatever you were doing in your own stubborn, independent way. And Koreans will react the same way to assertive American women—or their sympathetic husbands.

The foreign woman who accepts the "halfway between 'man' and 'woman' position" she will find herself in will discover there is virtually no place she cannot go, nothing she cannot do, and no limit to the Korean friends, both male and female, she can make.

The Importance of Proper Behavior

In Korea nothing signifies one's high status more surely than one's dress and one's polite way of acting in every situation. As a foreigner hoping to operate successfully in Korea, your appearance and self-presentation should always be that of a person of upper-class background—conservative in dress and well-bred, moderate, and courteous in behavior.

Excessive politeness at all times is the mark of proper behavior. Dignified gentlemen (or gentlewomen) must maintain that dignity at all times, never letting their guard down. Besides *dignified*, the words that can best be used to describe such a person are *reserved, unhurried, deliberate, calm, patient,* and *temperate* (except when dealing with the lowest of servants).

Koreans, of course, have been trained in how to act politely (Korean style) since birth; you, as a newcomer, have not. That is why so much effort (and such minute detail) has been given in this book to teach you how to act in the "proper" manner in polite Korean society. As you read the rest of this chapter, you are likely to wonder why I have gone to such lengths for what you will doubtlessly consider to be minor situations, but minor though they may seem, they will indicate to well-bred Koreans that you have also had a proper upbringing.

Throughout all levels of society, ceremony, formality, and ritual are taken very seriously and are likely to be applied in the simplest day-to-day social situations. Everything is done by a prescribed procedure, and it is considered less than polite to vary from those daily routines. Of course, all cultures have their ritualistic behaviors, but Koreans seem to be among the most ritually inclined, while Americans, individualists all, are among the least. This makes for good news and bad news. The bad news is that Americans are likely to chafe at the need to conform to unaccustomed routines in precisely the exact way everyone else does. The good news is that (1) the routines are performed consistently and without deviation, so that the person who wishes to adapt to living in Korea can take a relatively easy but major step by learning and following the rituals "to the letter," and (2) the rituals can be learned by simply observing and imitating the predictable, everyday, customary behaviors of your Korean hosts.

One particularly interesting aspect of proper behavior, which reveals one's high status, I have dubbed "assumed humility" or "one-downsmanship." Put simply, it is play-acting that everyone who is your equal is your superior, whether he or she is or not. It consists of downplaying your own accomplishments as absolutely disgraceful or shameful while at the same time exaggerating and lauding the accomplishments of your counterpart. The recipient of that praise, of course, is then expected to deny staunchly all of the compliments being received and to heap equally exaggerated praise on the other.

Nevertheless, though warned, it can be pretty unnerving the first time you, as an American, are invited to a Korean counterpart's home for dinner. As you sit down to eat, it immediately becomes obvious that the man's accomplished wife has labored skillfully over the meal for days (not hours). Yet the husband says something like "Oh, my poor wife. I'm so embarrassed by her. She's just a country girl and she doesn't know how to do anything right." But you must remember not to be embarrassed by his callousness, and don't punch the guy in the nose! Remember it's just a game, and now it is your move. Simply deny everything he has just said and heap as many compliments as you can think of on his home and his wife's cooking.

Another means of deprecating oneself in the service of status is to indicate that the other person is superior to you by asking that person—even when first introduced—to become your teacher. The Korean custom is to call everyone except the lowest of the low by the word *teacher* (*sŏnseng*) rather than "Mr.," "Miss," or "Mrs." It is a great compliment and show of respect. Another sign of this sort of implied or exaggerated compliment is for one Korean to ask another as they are being introduced, "*Apuro, chal putak hamnida*" ("Sometime in the future, please allow me to ask favors of you").

Assumed humility also applies to seating arrangements. For example, when you are invited to dinner with a Korean family, your host will indicate where you are to sit. As a neophyte in Korea, you are likely to follow directions. Wrong. If you were a Korean in such a situation, you would refuse, acting as though the seat you have been assigned is far too honorable a place for someone as lowly as you to take. Your host, also following the ritual, would continue to insist and you would continue to refuse, until you were eventually forced, physically if necessary, to sit in the honored spot.

Similarly, it is a mark of polite behavior and good Korean breeding to ignore the first offer of any courtesy invitation or request, whether it be to enter a room, sit down, receive a gift, or simply start eating. Polite Koreans will say *ne* (yes) the first and second time they are asked to do so, but they will not begin to follow through and actually do what is asked until asked at least three times. Only then, finally, will they act on the offer—reluctantly.

Still another tricky practice that is related to a show of humility is the way a polite person responds to a compliment, which is to deny it vigorously. In the United States, if you tell me I have a beautiful necktie, my proper response is to say "Thank you," indicating an appreciation for your recognition of my good taste. The proper Korean response is to say something like "What? This old tie? Oh, no, I've spilled so much food on it and it's so ugly, I'm ashamed to wear it." Although among Americans we might also disparage a personal compliment, it is not considered courteous to do so.

Here is an important one: it was the custom in Korea two or three decades ago that when someone admired something you owned, you gave it to the admirer. Many unwary Americans have suffered the embarrassment of being given or at least offered and urged, even forced, to accept some valuable if not irreplaceable possession of their hosts after having admired it, so be careful. You have been warned. And while it is unlikely to happen today, polite, well-bred Koreans would still be less likely to praise someone else's belongings than would their American counterparts.

Terms of Address and Introductions

Koreans refer to each other by title or by title and surname and rarely by given name alone. Following this ritual of proper behavior is important, partly because it is an appropriate way to honor your addressee and partly because in Korea one's given name is considered to be one's personal property, not to be used indiscriminately outside the family and in official communications. If you don't know the person's title, then, as we've noted, use the generic term, *sŏnseng*. If the person is elderly, referring to him or her as grandfather or grandmother is the appropriate, respectful form. When names are used, the surname comes first, which, incidentally, is another indication of the importance of the family (group) over the individual.

The only exception to never calling an adult Korean by his or her first (i.e., given) name would be a situation in which you already knew the person in an informal relationship, perhaps as a fellow student at an American university. You will meet Koreans who have spent time in the United States and who are familiar with American customs. If they ask you to call them by their given name or by a nickname they picked up while they were in the States, feel free to follow their invitation if you like, but be aware that doing so is out of place in Korea. The typical Korean way of reacting to such an invitation would be to show delight at the suggestion, offer profuse thanks for being given such a special privilege, do it once or twice, and then quietly revert to using the surname thereafter, along with the honorific *teacher* (e.g., Lee Sŏnseng). One interesting side note that you are not likely to discover on your own is that the Koreans love to give everyone within their group a nickname, but not reveal it to the person so named. Instead, they use it secretly among themselves. Should you discover the nickname for someone you know, you will be amazed at how appropriate it is.

There are only about 250 different family names in Korea, and three of those are the most common, with Kim securely in the lead. When you first arrive in Korea, it will seem that every other person you meet will be a "Mr. Kim" (the other two are Lee and Pak). Introductions in Korea assume a level of importance far beyond what Americans are accustomed to, because Koreans establish the rank and status of someone when they are introduced for the first time. They generally start off by asking a few key questions such as "Where is your place of origin?" (indicating which branch of the Kim family a person comes from), "What university did you attend?" and other such questions.

The small talk that follows introductions among Koreans consists of those topics that will provide them with the information they need to rank the other person without invading that person's privacy. This is especially tricky with Asians, who are less inclined than Westerners to reveal or, as do many Americans, readily describe (or boast of) their status and past achievements.

As discussed earlier, Koreans are most anxious to know about your place of origin, the school you graduated from, and your age. By place of origin (*kohyang*), they do not mean where your family now resides or simply the place where you were born; they mean the city to which your family traces its beginnings. The place of one's family's origin is especially dear to Koreans.

The question of what university you graduated from is, as mentioned, critical. Obviously, for Americans an identification with an Ivy League or other prestigious university or college in the United States is advantageous, as is any kind of graduate study or higher degree.

Do not be surprised if you are asked your age. Remember, as we discussed earlier, Koreans have exactly the opposite reaction to age that Americans typically do. In the United States the younger you are, the better. In Korea, it works the other way—the older you can claim to be, the greater prestige you have and the more credit and respect you are given. If you want to get the most credit possible, you can give your age by Korean count. This will add either one or two years to your age, depending on when your birthday is. Koreans (except those who have adopted Western customs) pay no attention to the precise month and day of birth (except when they have their horoscope read). They consider everyone to be one year old at birth (counting the nine months in the womb), and everyone in Korea advances one year in age on New Year's Day. Thus, a baby born near the end of the year—receiving an extra year for the time in the womb and another year at the beginning of the new year—can be credited with being two years old when Americans would only calculate the age as two months.

Rules of proper behavior make it extremely difficult to meet a Korean without having a mutual friend to initiate the introduction. This can be done in each other's physical presence, via a note or letter from the friend, or even his or her calling card with a note scribbled on it that you can hand to the person you want to meet. Foreigners are allowed to break this rule more readily than Koreans and can strike up a casual acquaintanceship with people in public places, but if this is a contact you want to pursue, you will still probably follow up the meeting with a formal exchange of business cards and, later, with further contact.

Once brought together by the mutual acquaintance, the custom in Korea is for the two new acquaintances to introduce themselves to each other by saying simply, "Let's introduce ourselves" and then "My name is...," followed by "I am seeing you for the first time." As the two people reveal their names, they speak them so modestly low and fast and so slurred that the words are almost impossible to understand. Yet, it would be impolite for you to say, "I'm sorry, I didn't catch your name. Would you please repeat it?" Luckily, at the same moment, they are handing each other a name card, conveniently turned right side up so that it is readable. Fortunately, most Korean professionals today have their cards translated into English on the reverse side. At the same moment as the two people give and receive each other's cards—offering and accepting them with both hands to be most polite—they each step backward half a step and bow slightly to the other. This bow is held a little longer than the average bow of greeting.

If you find yourself in this situation, it would be impolite to grab the card and stuff it into your pocket too quickly. Protocol calls for you to study it intently and make appropriate small gasps of astonishment and wordless exclamations which indicate you are appropriately impressed with the other person's high position or the important company he is employed by. Failing to engage properly in this little ritual will be taken as an insult by some Koreans.

At this point the mutual friend reinserts him- or herself into the process and gives each (in the proper highly exaggerated Korean way) a quick rundown of the wondrous achievements of the other person, who is, of course, too modest to recite them.

If you watch closely while Koreans go through this ritual, you will notice that the depth at which each of them bows will differ slightly. What they are doing is bowing at exactly the correct depth appropriate to their relative rank or position. This is a difficult subtlety, and it is not necessary for you to engage in it with precision at first. In fact, it may be that almost all Koreans in the circles in which you move will shake hands with you in the Western manner instead of bowing. Even more likely they will probably do both simultaneously.

You too, by the way, should have calling cards translated into Korean on one side. Luckily, it can be done in a day or two in any Korean print shop, though you might want to have them printed before you leave the United States (at a Korean print shop in cities like Washington, D.C., New York, Chicago, or Los Angeles), because you are likely to need them the moment you arrive.

Other Aspects of Proper Behavior

Americans might think it strange, but one aspect of proper behavior Koreans consider extremely important is posture. Koreans are much more formal than Americans in this respect. Informal stances and sitting positions are considered to be improper and even disrespectful to the other person, especially one of the positions American males have a proclivity for: slouching in a chair—almost lying—with legs spread and crossed with one ankle resting on the other knee. When you can, follow the Korean way of sitting—often stiff and extremely erect, with legs together and both feet flat on the floor. In traditional times, sitting directly on the floor in a normal position in front of an elder male was not allowed. Instead, the person was expected to kneel before him with both legs extended out behind and to stay in that position until urged three times to sit more comfortably (and not every elder was considerate enough to do the urging). Even today, before elders, young people are expected to sit upright, preferably on the edge of the chair, legs together, and with both feet planted firmly on the floor.

A final mark of proper behavior, one that Koreans feel is of major importance, is judging people by the company they keep. As egalitarians, Americans tend to find this a difficult restriction. Indeed, Americans have a worldwide reputation for talking to taxi drivers they have never seen before and will likely never see again or carrying on conversations with waiters as if they were their equals. If you observe yourself when you are at a restaurant, chances are you will have said thank you to the waiter at least three times before he or she brings your dinner. A thank-you is not something a Korean (or for that matter, a European) would often say to a waiter, who is, after all, "only a servant" and in no way considered to be an equal. (This is less true among younger, more modern Koreans today.)

****

The skill involved in adapting to several of the cultural traits discussed in this chapter and the previous one is called by intercultural specialists "dealing with ambiguity." Relaxing and cultivating an easygoing attitude that enables you to manage ambiguous situations will contribute substantially to your success in adapting to Korean culture. Look at the process as an intricate puzzle to be worked out slowly, over time, rather than as a barrier to accomplishing what you wish, and certainly not as something that Koreans have specifically designed to drive you stark raving mad.

8

Relationships: Ingroups and Outgroups

Recall our discussions of Critical Incidents 2 and 5, which illustrate how Koreans divide people quite rigidly into insiders and outsiders. Insiders, starting with your blood relatives and including all of the people with whom you are affiliated—through the schools you attended, your place of work, your military unit, church, province or city of origin, and so on—are the only people who matter, who deserve any of your care, attention, and response. It is those groups of people with whom you have established an ingroup relationship for whom no sacrifice is too great.

Koreans often comment, as we have pointed out in Critical Incident 6, that Americans treat their friends like strangers and strangers like friends. They cannot understand how we can be so friendly to people we do not know and how we can have anything less than total dedication to a friend. Part of the explanation for this disparity in outlook lies in a fundamental difference in how human society is perceived.

To Americans society is a collection of individuals. To Koreans it is a collection of groups. As Americans, we are likely to feel that family ties in the United States are quite strong, until we begin to compare them with family ties in most of the rest of the world. It is basic to the American value system to view the individual as having the rights of self-expression, self-realization, and self-protection, even though these rights may conflict with the interests of the family as defined by society. Americans join other groups, attend schools, and work in organizations, but the relationships they develop in these contexts are relatively weak and do not stir binding loyalties. Social and geographic mobility has, from the very beginning of the U.S., been such a part of the daily life of Americans, and the breaking of ties with friends, identity groups, and even family members is such a common experience, that Americans have gotten used to maintaining loose ties with their ingroups and easily develop skills in relating to strangers.

Insiders

In Korea the family is the primary ingroup, fount of love, trust, loyalty, and protection. It also involves obedience. The father is traditionally the family's unquestioned head, ruling with near absolute authority according to the design of Confucianism, where the most important relationships refer to the family: husband, wife; father, son; older and younger brothers. We have noted in chapter 7 the significance of age, the great degree of respect given to elders in the family and the importance of age in brother-to-brother relationships. We also discussed the status of the wife. Sons were destined to maintain the lineage, the family name, and the strength of the family group. The eldest son had the responsibility for caring for his parents in their old age, for as long as they lived. There is an old belief in Korea, still widely held, that if parents die young it is the fault of the children—a belief likely to make children solicitous of their parents' health and well-being.

The Korean family is not merely the nuclear family on which Americans place so much significance, nor is it limited to the extended family important among Latins and Arabs, though, of course, Korea's is an extended family system. It is all of these plus the lineage of the family. Upper-class Koreans have family registers that not only list all of one's known ancestors as far into the distant past as they can be identified but also project ahead by indicating the names of the male offspring for five or ten generations into the future.

The most important relatives, of course, are one's direct-line ancestors. Americans are familiar with the Confucian practice often mistakenly referred to as "ancestor worship." A more accurate term and one less likely to cause offense to American religious beliefs is ancestor *veneration*. Besides its intrinsic value, one's practice of filial piety is an indicator of the person's true worth, measuring the respect he or she shows for deceased parents and other ancestors.

In the old days, up to seventy-five to one hundred years ago, the period of mourning for one's parents was three years— and thirty years for the whole country when the king died! White (not black as in Europe and the U.S.) is the traditional color of mourning. It is said that the reason white is presently the most popular color for clothing, especially in rural Korea, whether one is in mourning or not, is because people got so used to wearing white during the long periods of royal mourning.

Another indication of the importance of family in Korea is the large number of terms referring to family-member relationships. These terms become extremely specific, with a different word assigned to each. A woman's eldest brother, for example, rates his own descriptive nomenclature, not merely the couple of adjectives added to a noun that English calls for. Where English has no more than two dozen words to identify all of our relatives, one author counted 181 terms used to denote family relationships in Korean* (e.g., *haraboji*,

---

* A special appendix in Paul Crane's *Korean Patterns* (Seoul: Royal Asiatic Society Korea Branch, 1986) offers a complete list of the Korean words and the relationships they identify.

the most familiar form when addressing one's grandfather; *chobo*, formal, speaking to or about one's grandfather; and *wangbujang*, speaking to others about their grandfather).

As should be amply clear by now, in Korea a great deal of importance is placed on creating and perpetuating families. Unmarried foreign men and women will be hounded by repeated questions as to why they are not married, and childless couples will be asked over and over again why they have no children. No answer that is comprehensible to Koreans has yet been discovered.

The next major component of one's ingroup consists of friends. As we've already noted in Critical Incident 6, the Korean concept of friendship is strikingly different from that of Americans. Ask average Americans how many friends they have and they are likely to tell you a large number. Ask average Koreans how many friends they have and they are likely to say one or perhaps two. Koreans develop close and deep relationships with their one or two intimate friends. Most of those whom Americans call their friends are more accurately described in Korea as acquaintances.

The relationship Koreans have with their one or two truly close friends is one of complete sharing of time, feelings, material possessions, and all of the other intimate aspects of their lives. By Korean definition, the obligations of friendship are heavy indeed. Most Americans value their privacy too much to allow such a burdensome closeness and complete sharing. Another interesting (and revealing) difference between Koreans and Americans is that Americans often want to introduce their friends to each other and get them together on social occasions. Koreans, on the other hand, may be less willing to introduce one friend to another. This difference depends on whether you believe, as Americans do, that there are a limitless number of potential friendships out there, or whether, as Koreans believe, true friends are in limited supply, like every other commodity in the world.

This is a very important point, since it should be clear that unless there is some specific reason for you to become transformed from an outsider to an insider, you should not expect Koreans, from their point of view, to want to get to know you—they already have enough obligations with their current friends.

Once you are considered to be a friend (in the Korean meaning of the word), however, no request is too expensive or too impossible (and perhaps even too illegal) to ask. By Korean definition a friend is someone you can call at three o'clock in the morning and say, "Can you come over right away and bring five hundred dollars" and that person does not say, "It's the middle of the night! Besides, I don't know if I've got the cash" or even ask why you need it in such a rush, but says, "I'll be right there with the money." (It would embarrass me to call even my wife at that hour with such a request unless I had an airtight explanation ready.) With that kind of expectation, you can see why Koreans would be unlikely to claim more than one or two friends. So if you should be so fortunate as to be invited into an ingroup, you need to be willing and prepared to handle such requests. Simply saying it is impossible or illegal for you to do what is asked will not put an end to the matter. It will only bring the response, "Yes, I know it is impossible. I know you cannot do it, but please do it anyway." In some cases, saying something is impossible to do may only give the impression you are holding out for a bribe (or for a larger bribe if one has already been offered; see chapter 9 for more on the bribery implications of this phenomenon). Also keep in mind, as discussed in chapter 6, that one should not use an outright no. The proper Korean way to refuse is to affect an extremely pained expression and to explain that it would be very difficult for you to do *at this time*, keeping your explanation sufficiently ambiguous, indefinite, and open-ended. Such a refusal, which has the virtue of avoiding loss of face, will work, but it will also, in all probability, end the close relationship.

Among even the closest friends, sometimes misunderstandings and fights occur. When they do, they will require arbitrators to restore the relationship. But the go-between must be permitted to operate in the Korean rather than the American manner. The American go-between would in all likelihood bring the alienated friends together in a three-person meeting. The Korean way is to have the arbitrator meet privately with each person, going back and forth between the two until the conflict has finally been resolved. In this way, face has been preserved on both sides.

Americans need personal time, time to be alone, away from their family and their best friends (even by the Korean definition). Privacy is considered by Americans to be almost a sacred right. Koreans cannot understand this characteristic of Americans. In the context of their strong group orientation, being left to oneself is an almost unbearable condition. What someone needs when alone is to be cheered up by friends, in order that his or her kibun might be restored. The word used for *privacy* in Korean is extremely negative, carrying with it the connotation that the person, alone and lonely, has been driven out of the group. It is almost impossible for a Korean to comprehend that *privacy* means exactly the opposite to Americans. In Korea, true friends read each other's personal letters without asking permission and without being thought of as violating the right to privacy that Americans believe is their due no matter what the relationship.

Comparable is the difference between Americans and Koreans in ideas about ownership. When a Korean borrows a personal possession from a friend, he or she does not consider the item to be on a short-term loan. Borrowing is much more permanent for Koreans. The American who lends the object should realize that the lender must be the one to ask to "borrow" the item back if and when he or she needs it again.

Although the dividing line between acquaintances and friends is different, there is a distinction between true friends and friends as acquaintances in both countries. Both Koreans and Americans develop a range of acquaintanceships that fall short of friendship. In Korea these relationships play a critical role in the social and economic affairs of the country, since they serve as a source of introductions and are all-important in initiating useful personal contacts.

School relationships are particularly fertile ground for the development of these kinds of acquaintanceships, which are renewed every time alumni happen to meet. Bonds between especially close classmates last a lifetime. Koreans who preceded you in graduating from your school are always deferred to, and graduates from the same schools are not reluctant to make use of the vast networks these institutions automatically provide. There is always someone among them who can serve as the link to help you contact the right person and even persuade that person to say yes to your request.

For you, such networks already in existence might include the Korean alumni of your American university(ies); community organizations such as Rotary International (in which you will have wisely taken out a membership before leaving the States); your church denomination or fellow congregants; pastors of nearby Korean churches in the United States; your local chamber of commerce; Korean affiliates of trade associations† and professional groups in your industry; Korean businessmen in your community at home; U.S. companies with branches in Korea, even though their companies are not your own (contacts in the U.S. may have contacts there); and any other sources that have potential. Another potential network for you is established if you volunteer to teach an English class or tutor an individual. This can often be your

---

† There are several organizations in Korea that have been formed to assist the foreign businessperson, such as the American Chamber of Commerce in Seoul; the Korean Chamber of Commerce and Industry (KCCI) in Seoul; the Korean Exhibition Center (KOEX), an international trade show and convention center; and the Korean World Trade Center (KWTC); and in major U.S. cities, The Korea Trade Center (KOTRA).

ticket, in the future, to creating a new network of your own to receive return contacts and favors, Korean style. From each prospect you can identify, you should ask for a brief letter of introduction, particularly if the writer is a friend or close acquaintance of the hoped-for contact. You will be surprised to discover how easily doors will open to you in Korea as a result of a hand-carried letter of introduction from a mutual acquaintance or friend. At least obtain general "To whom it may concern" letters, which, interestingly, are much more effective in Korea than they are in the U.S. In all these ways you can build your own Korean networks.

One option, especially for the younger person or couple, is to work at developing a close relationship with a Korean family and then at the right moment ask if they would become your Korean mother and Korean father—if, in essence, they would "adopt" you into their family. If done properly and at the opportune time, they will be so touched by the request that they will be unable to refuse. The only difficulty I experienced in having established such a relationship was that now, being the "American son" of a respectable Korean family, I was expected to associate no longer with a whole range of lower-status people with whom, as an American, I felt a desire or need to develop relationships (including Buddhist monks, who have been out of favor and looked down on since the late Koryŏ Dynasty in the fourteenth century). My need to connect as a Korean ingroup member, however, overcame my American egalitarian impulses.

By now it should be clear that if, while working in Korea, you happen to develop a close friendship with a Korean, then his or her whole network of acquaintances and contacts will automatically become accessible to you. Koreans are among the best networkers in the world, and since they are not the least bit hesitant about using your connections, you shouldn't be about using theirs.

One result of this strong orientation toward family and friend ingroup identification is a pervasive nepotism in Korean society. Since this subject is discussed in the comments to Critical Incident 8, I only want to briefly mention here something I call "false nepotism." Koreans will introduce someone to you as a brother or sister without telling you they are not really a blood relative. This additional information may (or may not) over time be leaked to you, but the assumption appears to be that you will be impressed by the fact that the person you are meeting is a relative of the person doing the introducing; in other words, that you, too, place positive value on nepotistic connections.

Finally, Koreans do have affiliations beyond those with family, friends, and school (and sometimes military) friends. They belong to or join other kinds of groups: social, office, religious, political, and so forth. They tend, however, to be much more cautious in checking out the group's history and current membership than the typical American would be. Nevertheless, once having done so and having found it safe, the Koreans would be more likely than the American to stay in the organization for a longer time.

Outsiders

Given Koreans' strong feelings about insiders, it should not be surprising to find their attitudes toward outsiders equally clear—they are, in fact. Everyone who is not identified as ingroup through a personal affiliation of some sort is to be ignored as if they did not exist. Outsiders have nothing to do with you, and you have no obligation whatsoever to them. Therefore, the rude Korean businessman in Critical Incident 2 and Mr. Pak's callous reaction to a poor Korean mother and child in Critical Incident 5 must be understood within the outgroup context.

Outgroups may be seen as falling into at least three categories:

1. The low classes in the Confucian hierarchy: beggars, prostitutes, waitresses (who in earlier days were thought to be

easily available for hired sex after working hours), criminals, and servants;

2. All of the people in the world with whom one does not
   have an established relationship; and

3. Foreigners in Korea, who have come to make up a class of
   their own because there have been so many of them in
   the country in recent years.

Concerning the first group, those outcasts at the very bottom of the heap, most Koreans have absolutely no contact
with or feelings about them. To the vast majority of Koreans,
these unfortunate people do not exist (this is the relevant
factor in Critical Incident 5).

The second classification, by definition, includes almost
everyone else, including Koreans not in one's ingroup. Even
if one wanted to, one would never have the chance to interact with more than a handful of those strangers. In countries
as overpopulated as most Asian countries are, one normally
does not have a desire to meet more people.

One pronounced behavioral pattern resulting from the
Koreans' feelings about outgroup members is a distinct "me
first" attitude toward anyone who is unknown to them. If you
experience having a Korean grab a taxi out from under you
when you had obviously hailed it first (as happens in Critical
Incident 2) or push ahead of you to get on a bus or subway
car, or shove ahead of you in a store, you will understand the
power of this attitude. Dealing with this kind of behavior
may be one of the greatest challenges you have in coming to
terms with living in Korea. Of course, Koreans treat each
other this way also; it's not just you—or not just foreigners.

As is the case in many if not most societies, people look
down on those from other provinces or regions—and urbanites in Seoul look down on them all. Koreans can recite a
verse composed by a Confucian scholar, Lee Twap-Gye, about
five hundred years ago, that assigns specific attributes to the
people who come from each of the various provinces of Ko-

rea. All of the attributions are stereotypes, and most of them are uncomplimentary, but every Korean has memorized the verses, and most of them believe there is truth in these stereotypes.

While not all Americans are known for their skills at empathizing with other people, you will be struck by the general lack of empathy or sympathy Koreans show toward anyone who is not an ingroup member. The Korean attitude toward those with physical disabilities or deformities seems particularly cruel and uncaring. Widows, orphans, and racially-mixed and/or illegitimate children fare little better. Ingroup social norms offer security to group members, but sometimes at a high social cost.

Attitudes toward Foreigners

The attitude of Koreans toward foreigners in general may, to some, seem not to have progressed far from that of the Chinese Imperial Court where (and this continued until late in the nineteenth century) the Chinese Foreign Office was called the Ministry of Barbarian Affairs. To be fair, foreigners in Korea often have a rather unique though relatively recent status, that of half-guest, half-outsider, which means you may receive a little more recognition than the other two groups of outsiders, though not a great deal more. This is especially possible for foreigners who give evidence of being "sincere" and dress as though they are from the upper class. They will even be expected and allowed to make mistakes as long as they are obviously endeavoring to learn to do things the Korean way. Foreign women, especially those who are accompanied by their husbands, will often be given status superior to that of Korean women and permitted to accompany their husbands to events where Korean wives are normally excluded.

Americans in Korea constitute a special case, and attitudes toward them tend to be somewhat ambivalent. On the one

hand, they are associated with the presence, for over fifty
years, of forty thousand American troops (who strike some
Koreans the way American GIs did the British in World War
II: "overpaid, overfed, oversexed, and over here!"). At least
some Korean students who have studied in the United States
have returned with strong negative feelings about American
culture and U.S. international political and economic domination. Most Koreans who have studied in the U.S. usually
have a positive attitude toward Americans, however, and
most who have not yet been to the U.S. to study would give
their eyeteeth to be able to do so.

The U.S. soldiers in Korea are there because the United
States is South Korea's ally in the enduring (though, hope-
fully, lessening) confrontation with North Korean commu-
nism. And while American economic and political power is
mistrusted, on the other side of the coin is the fact that
economic aid from the U.S. has played a major role in driving
Korea's industrial and technological development.

Koreans' ambivalent perceptions of the United States are
in large part generational. The older generations still look
toward the U.S. with gratitude for its soldiers having liberated Korea from the Japanese at the end of World War II and
coming to their aid in the Korean War and for the American
economic aid that boosted Korea's war-torn economy. The
rise of anti-Americanism among younger Koreans dates from
the mid-1980s and is less strong at the time of this writing
than it was earlier, although this is an attitude that readily
fluctuates depending on the current political climate. Below
are two diametrically opposed opinions of the U.S., one in
the voice of an elderly Korean man, the other, of a Korean
college student.

The older man:
    I believe I am in no way unique. I represent all
    Koreans of my generation, the generation that

experienced the humiliation of the Japanese occupation of Korea and the exhilaration of the American liberation in 1945. This performance was repeated once more when thousands of young American soldiers came to Korea—thirty thousand of them to die on Korean soil—to help us fight to avoid a takeover by the aggressor North Koreans. For these two acts alone, Koreans should be eternally grateful to the Americans.

It is to the Americans, too, that Korea owes its present economic success, for the knowhow and the millions of dollars in U.S. aid America poured into Korea. But many young Koreans, who weren't born when these things happened, have become openly hostile to the Americans.

The American missionaries who came to Korea to risk their lives in order to carry their message to my grandparents represent yet another reason we should be grateful to the Americans, who brought us not only the Christian religion but also our first universities and hospitals as well as human rights and welfare concerns.

For these reasons, we Koreans should be in perpetual debt to the Americans for what they have done and continue to do for Korea. Like a student who is eternally thankful to his professor for giving him his knowledge, the Americans will always be our mentors.

It is only out of ignorance and shameful rudeness that some of today's Korean students openly criticize the Americans and attempt to drive them out of our country.

The young Korean‡:

I am truly ashamed of my father and his generation for their spineless, obsequious attitude toward the Americans, considering the shameful acts they continue to inflict upon us. Their legacy, the half-breed Korean-American children their soldiers fathered and left on Korean soil to remind us forever of their presence here, gives me a renewed sense of shame every day of my life.

My father and his whining generation continue to bow to the Americans, and they continue to beg them to stay here to continue their rape of our women. The record is clear, in spite of the fact that the Americans have done their level best to hide what they have done, but let the record speak for itself.

Most Americans and many Koreans do not realize it, but it is an indisputable fact that the Americans were directly responsible for the horrendous and ignoble occupation of Korea from 1910 to 1945 by the Japanese warlords. Their president, Theodore Roosevelt, in the Taft-Katsura Agreement signed on American soil, allowed the Japanese to take over Korea in exchange for the Japanese remaining silent about the Americans having recently taken over the Philippines. This act became Korea's burden and national disgrace.

At the end of World War II, as U.S. troops moved into southern Korea to liberate Korea from the Japanese and to free Korea from the Japanese Colonial Empire, they permitted the

‡ This view was especially strong in the 1980s.

Soviets to move into northern Korea *just one week before the end of the war*. This foolish act (already agreed upon between the Russians and the Americans at Yalta) sealed the humiliating division between North and South Korea that exists to this day!

At the time of liberation, in 1945, the American military powers asked the Japanese warlords to remain in Korea to continue as our leaders, although they had just been defeated. You cannot imagine the shame, humiliation, anger, and resentment that this unforgivable act kindled in the hearts and minds of every patriotic Korean. They wanted to humiliate us even further and prolong our anguish and shame. For this act alone, I can never forgive the Americans!

The American victors helped the new Korean leadership create the Korean CIA modeled after that of the U.S. The Korean CIA is responsible for the imprisonment and murder of thousands of our most loyal Korean citizens over the last fifty years.

The Kwanju Massacre[§] of 1980, during which Korean troops ruthlessly murdered hundreds of our brave Korean youth, can ultimately be blamed not only on the Korean military but on the American general who, as a commander of the United Nations forces in Korea, would have had to have given his permission to allow Korean troops to move in to commit their murderous acts. The blood of

---

[§] Of all of the young Korean's charges, this one is the least substantiated. It is doubtful, in fact, that American permission was given, but radical-minded Koreans say that such large-scale troop movement would have had to be approved by the American government.

these brave martyrs will never wash off the hands of the Americans who gave the cowardly order!

From the very beginning of our liberation from the Japanese, the American government has continued to support and give financial backing to the dictators we have had as presidents: from Syngman Rhee through Park Chung Hee, Chun Doo Hwan, and Roh Tae Woo.

No, I will never be able to forgive the Americans for what they have done to Korea and the Korean people—from the beginning of the century to this very day! Go home Yankees! And the sooner the better!

There are of course no simple responses to these charges. Fortunately, they are not as common today as they were a decade ago, but they are still to be found. Political debates of this sort are inevitable in international relations, and one must arm oneself as best one can. Certainly negotiating these as well as all the other cross-cultural land mines we've discussed so far in this book is a challenge to the sensitive visitor, but one well worth the effort, since actively endeavoring to come to terms with radically different perspectives offers the best route to both a rewarding experience and the accomplishment of the goals which took you abroad in the first place.

9

Paths to Success, Korean Style

Education

One of the most effective ways of advancing oneself in Korea has been education. This has been true for the past five hundred years. What has changed is that then one had to be the son of a yangbang to qualify, and one's education would be limited to the Confucian classics. Now anyone who is academically qualified can aspire to a university degree or beyond. A college education, and especially graduate degrees, enable people to rise rapidly beyond the restrictions that would otherwise be imposed upon them by their lower- and lower-middle-class status. The diplomas and degrees, however, do not come cheaply or without competition. To succeed one has to be accepted into the right schools, whether in Korea or in the United States. But in order to get into the right university, one has to have graduated from the right high school. In order to do that, one must come from the right middle school, and so on all the way back to the right kindergarten. Competition has become increasingly keen and the entrance exams harder and harder, resulting in a phenomenon similar to the "exam hell" for which Japan is so notorious. Once accepted into the best Korean university that will accept you, the game is won. It is no longer necessary to study very seriously in order to graduate, and the graduates of the best schools were always, prior to the economic crisis of 1997 and 1998, snatched up by the largest and most prestigious companies.

Some observers note that this system of ceasing to work hard after high school is gradually changing, but there still seems to be a great disparity between the amount of work expected from students in Korean universities and the amount expected in U.S. institutions of higher learning. In general U.S. universities require much more in the way of individual research and written papers than is expected in Korea. Academic requirements are still heavier and more strictly enforced, class attendance and participation are expected, and English has to be mastered. Studying in an American university, therefore, sometimes poses great challenges for Korean students, who are accustomed to taking it easy during university study. Nonetheless, thousands have made it through, and in returning to Korea they have found that, as a reward, they have advanced much more rapidly in their careers. In fact, education is now *the* most important requirement for establishing one's status in Korea, followed by family background, the status of one's hometown, and that of the school one graduated from.

Never Take No for an Answer

As you begin to make friends and acquaintances in Korea, you will probably find that some of them might even try to involve you in helping them meet their goals, and occasionally you would be well advised to consider whether to comply or not (and if not, how you might best extricate yourself with the least possible damage). This admonition is doubly necessary because, as I have tried to illustrate, your reasoned cause-and-effect logic will be totally useless in explaining why something is impossible for you to do.

One of the surest keys to functioning successfully in Korea

is understanding the complex procedures by which Koreans pursue what they want. The Korean saying quoted earlier merits restatement, since you will hear it over and over again: "Yes, I know it cannot be done, but please do it anyway" or the more generalized statement, "Everything is impossible... and everything is possible." These were the automatic responses I heard hundreds of times from Koreans after I had explained, I thought very carefully and very thoroughly, why it was utterly impossible for me to do whatever incredible thing they had just asked me to do.

Any halfway intelligent person, I believed, would eventually learn from these long, logical reasons I had just given to justify my stand that there was no use in pursuing the matter further. Not my Korean supplicants! Nothing other than giving them what they asked for would have been acceptable. But the real lesson I learned from those experiences was that my "logical," legalistic reasoning had, in the Korean context, no validity whatsoever. It was merely, for the Koreans, a lame excuse. I might as well have said as my reason, "I cannot fulfill your request because the magpie is black and white." It would have made as much sense and seemed almost as appropriate as all my Aristotelian logic.

The important thing to understand here is that this is not simply a curious quirk in the Korean personality. It is part of a complex sociopsychological mindset that constitutes the Korean way of handling the universal human need to pursue one's own self-interest in a society that does not encourage individual advancement. It is also the result of hundreds of years of servitude to others and of having learned that one must be persistent if one is to get ahead at all.

From one perspective, and one that is particularly disturbing to Americans, regulations and reasons in Korea are only used as the first line of defense in refusing a request. Their monomaniacal persistence in this context was a signal to me that what they were asking without saying it precisely was "What would it really take for you to comply with my request? I'm willing to negotiate" and then "How much money are you demanding?" In other words, it was part of a ritual of negotiating an informal fee-for-services agreement, commonly (in this kind of situation) referred to as a bribe.

"Bribery"

There are many ways of accomplishing the impossible in Korea, and to say "It cannot be done" is really only to communicate the idea that you are holding out for a bribe or for a larger bribe than has already been offered. But to make a moral judgment on the process and take a rigid stand on the basis of your belief in right and wrong will both miss the point and substantially reduce your effectiveness in Korea. There are ways to make the system work for you that avoid a moral impasse (and that sidestep the issue of trespassing American law, which is not advised). If I may be allowed, a couple of incidents out of my own experience will illustrate my point.

Once, on a brief business trip to Seoul, I managed to squeeze in a side trip to visit an American friend in Taegu, my old stomping grounds. She asked me if there was anything in particular I wanted to see. I replied that I knew it was an impossible request, but that I had a strong desire to go to Kyŏngju, Korea's ancient capital during the Shilla Dynasty. I especially wanted to visit Pulguksa Temple. She agreed to drive me there. The fifty-mile trip took longer than we had expected, and we arrived after the temple was closed. But all that we needed to do was plead at length with the guard at the gate to allow us entry, using the sad story of how home-sick I was for the Korea I had not seen for several years and that this temple was the one site I wanted to revisit in all of Korea. Besides, it was such a beautiful, moonlit night, and I had never been able to view this temple in the moonlight before.

The guard relented. We were allowed to roam the temple grounds in the moonlight, and as we left, we gave the guard a modest tip, along with my endless thanks. Koreans making the same request would have slipped the money to the guard at the beginning of the negotiation and cut the time and the thank-yous considerably.

This incident illustrates the two principal ways of getting what you want in Korea:

1. Never take no for an answer.

2. Just keep talking until you have your way, even if the excuses you are able to think up don't sound particularly convincing to you. The point is to keep talking, no matter what, even if you merely repeat the same point over and over.

A second example occurred when I was headmaster of a vocational school in Korea. We were experiencing great difficulties in getting the school set up within our limited budget. Unfortunately, every time we acquired the basic equipment to add another area of vocational training, the tools would be stolen. But what was even more disheartening was knowing that the local police would do nothing to catch the criminals and get the tools back unless and until I first paid them a bribe, and the night watchman we had hired seemed unable to stop the thefts.

Paying a bribe, of course, did not fit into my U.S.-born ethical system. I worried a great deal and spent many sleepless nights trying to figure out how to solve the dilemma. It was especially troubling to me to know that the Korean police were very effective in solving such problems once properly compensated. The problem lay in my aversion to paying them a bribe to initiate the process.

During one of these sleepless nights, I finally came up with a solution that fit my moral stance and which could be bent to fit the Korean system as well. I would offer them a *reward* instead of a bribe. Now, the only significant difference between a bribe and a reward (or a tip, as in the first example) in this kind of situation is *when* you pay it, before or after the event. There is also the question of trust, that is, whether I am to be the one who trusts them by paying the money up front or whether they are forced to trust me to pay the money after they have returned the stolen goods.

It took much explaining by my Korean assistant, in private, to convince them to try this "strange American's way," but they finally agreed. They proved to be more trusting than I was prepared to be of them. They caught the thieves and forced them to return the tools and equipment. I paid the reward, and we never had any more thefts at the school.

When my wife and I departed for the States at the end of our three-year tour, the entire staff of the local police department lined the road to bow as we drove by on our way to the train station. "Everything is impossible...and everything is possible."

This example (as well as the first) illustrates a third way of getting what you want in Korea:

3. If all else fails, reinterpret the event.

At the Pulguksa Temple a bribe became a tip; at the school it became a reward—and both were within the ethical limitations I had brought with me to Korea.

As noted, the persevering refusal to accept no for an answer is not unique to Korea. It is found in many other cultures. But what does seem special is that in Korea this kind of aggressiveness and tenaciousness is combined with the indirect, passive, never-raise-your-voice-or-show-your-anger nature of the mild-mannered Korean. It may be that the extremity of Korean perseverance is related to life in a difficult environment where for centuries scarcity was a basic motivator and staying with the struggle was essential to surviving.

Nor is bribery unique to Korea, and the common garden variety is not that different from tipping. It simply involves a broadened definition of who deserves a tip. The usual justification for the pervasiveness of small bribes paid to lower-level government officials in order to facilitate paperwork and the issuance of permits—like that of waiters in the United States—is that the salaries they receive have been too low for them to live on. But here, too, things are changing. Bribery (or tips) is no longer necessary in order to get low-level officials to do their job. Large bribes, however, are still sometimes paid to high-level officials—usually to speed up the decision-making process. Koreans might still, on occasion, use bribes to get what they want (to a teacher, for example, to ensure one's children are not overlooked), to avoid something they don't want (e.g., to journalists, to avoid negative press about the chaebŏl [conglomerates]), or to keep out of trouble (e.g., to inspection officials from construction contractors).

Koreans often invite Americans to be their guests at a tearoom or coffeehouse to make requests for favors, which sometimes seem to Americans to be beyond the bounds of reason. The best response—as it is in so many situations in Korea—is to remain vague and ambiguous regarding the request (and avoid an outright refusal), but insist on picking up the bill. Since that would normally be the host's responsibility, you will, by violating the protocol, subtly convey that your answer is no without actually using the word.

Networking and "Pull"

People the world over expand their contacts through friends and acquaintances. What is uniquely Korean is the effectiveness of the networking system. And the good news is that even as a foreigner you can have access to the networks of any of your Korean contacts with whom you have already developed a reasonably good relationship. I urge you to plug into these networks with the assurance that your Korean contacts and co-workers will consider it a compliment that you see them as being so well connected and so powerful.

Since I have discussed networking in detail in chapter 8, please refer back to these pages (129–30).

Closely connected with networking is the procedure of finding people who will give you "pull" (*yongul*). In Korea, especially among those who are not graduates of the best universities and who are lacking powerful relatives, the need for proper introductions or pull is that much greater.

The importance of these kinds of contacts leads many Koreans to attach themselves to some powerful person for life, devoting themselves to supporting that individual for the personal benefits they will receive in return.

One of the results of this emphasis on the importance of pull is that Koreans who run their own business or anyone who has made it to a position of power and authority will be mobbed by members of his or her ingroup to either give or find them jobs. The average American would be driven to distraction by the time and energy demanded to respond to these incessant requests for help. The average Korean is not. The psychological rewards and enhancement of reputation that result for Koreans from such a visible manifestation of power seem to be ample compensation for the demands made upon them.

Gifts

Gift giving is a collateral sociocultural system somewhat similar in both its nature and its complexity to bribery. Gifts are sometimes given by Koreans for very much the same purpose as bribes, that is, with the aim of expecting favors in return. In this ambiguous context, bribes and gifts tend to merge so that they have to be redefined by size; true gifts are smaller, gifts intended as bribes are larger. If you have accepted a substantial gift and then refuse to say yes to the request for the favor that is certain to follow, you have, by Korean standards, been "insincere."

But how, specifically, do you distinguish a normal gift from one intended as a bribe? A good rule of thumb is this: if your immediate reaction is one of shock that this person is giving you a gift without any rationale for doing so and/or the gift is far too expensive to be reasonable under the circumstances, you should not accept it.

Alternatively, you might accept the gift and then recipro-cate with a gift of equal value the very same day. This could prove an expensive game to play, however. It is less risky to refuse to accept the gift with a statement like "This gift is far too expensive for me to accept," "I could never repay such an expensive gift," "It is not possible for me to accept this gift right now. I am sorry...," or something even more vague. The most important thing is to make it quite clear and be very definite that you are not accepting the gift—but never use the word *no*. That would be rude and offensive. The more ambiguity in your refusal, the better.

Normal gift giving follows patterns common to many cul-tures. Dinner guests in Korea often bring a small gift. A Korean friend who is familiar with American birthday cus-toms might give you a small birthday present. More signifi-cantly, if you are negotiating a commercial agreement with a Korean business or a collegial relationship with a Korean university, an exchange of reasonably priced gifts between the key officers is a normal part of the process. In such a case, gifts with your company's or your university's logo on it are especially appropriate.

Certain Korean gift-giving rules are quite different from those that are familiar to Americans. Normally, Koreans do not open the gift in front of the giver. Some will not say thank you or, if they do, they are not nearly as profuse or exaggerated in their thanks as Americans are expected to be. Gifts are always given and received using two hands and offering a slight bow. When bringing a small gift as a house present, Koreans usually deposit the gift inconspicuously just inside the door as they enter; then, as they are about to leave, they hand it, almost as an afterthought, to the host or hostess, and depart without the gift being opened in their presence. Gifts of money (which are appropriately given for such Korean occasions as weddings, funerals, and the newborn baby's "first 100-day" celebration) must always be enclosed in a white envelope.

Permanently employed household servants expect a monetary gift or tip when they are asked to provide services beyond those normally required by their job, for example, when a maid is asked to stay late to serve at a party.

In addition to the above ways Koreans have discovered to get what they want against enormous odds, there is still another ingenious method they have invented: the folk financial institution of the *kye*, devised to create an immediate pool of cash when suddenly required. Acquaintances and friends form a group whose members would like, when it is their turn, to have access to a fairly large sum of money to use for a specific period of time, say four to six months, before having to pay it back to the group. Each of a dozen or so kye members pays a predetermined amount to create a large pool of money. All of the members, in turn, will have access to the money for a personal project.

From time to time, one hears of a kye member absconding with the group's assets, but all told, the system is less risky than putting one's money into the lottery. Simple in concept, it is a fast way of increasing one or two thousand dollars to twenty-five thousand, which can then be invested in a project and later paid back for use by the next member.

Many ethnic Americans who have not known about this ingenious Korean invention have wrongly assumed that poor Korean immigrants have been favored over their own cultural group and been given government loans to begin their small mom-and-pop grocery stores, when it was really the Koreans' membership in a neighborhood kye that provided them the necessary collateral to start up their business.

****

As skilled as Koreans are at getting ahead, they are equally adept at accepting failure, hardship, and suffering—and at starting over again from zero. Compared with the average American, Koreans have a remarkable ability to adjust to whatever their present situation is. The reason, of course, is their acceptance of the idea that fate is the ultimate determinant of what happens to them, and it must be accepted with dignity. Given Korea's recent history—which includes the long period of Japanese rule (1910–1945), occupation by Americans (1945 to present) totally unfamiliar with Korea or any other Asian culture, and the Korean War (1950–1953) as well as the economic recession that began in late 1997, it is not surprising today to find successful Korean businessmen who have experienced three or four life calamities or total failures and yet have, each time, reached new personal heights in their recoveries. Knowing scores of Koreans who have made their way to the top again for the second, third, or even fourth time can only give one the utmost respect for their tenacity and for the sixteen-hour workdays they are willing to endure to rise again.

Negotiating with Koreans

Although the remaining chapters of this book appear to be addressed primarily to Americans who are going to be engaged in business in Korea or with Koreans in the United States, they apply to a wider audience. In whatever capacity you find yourself working in Korea or interacting with Koreans,* be assured that these chapters are for you and that the information they contain, while contextualized in a business setting, are applicable to your particular situation as well.

The first step in establishing a business or professional relationship with Koreans or in pursuing a Korean joint venture is seeking out, identifying, and making initial contact with a prospective partner. There are many channels—chambers of commerce, state economic development offices, businesses already operating in Korea, and so on—through which to make these initial explorations.

---

* And there are many: as a member of a U.S. military unit assigned to Korea, a Fulbright scholar or professor on a research or teaching assignment, a high school exchange student or college student, an international student adviser at an American university with students from Korea under your supervision, a volunteer assigned to one of the many religious agencies working in Korea, or a spouse accompanying someone employed by one of the above.

Let's start by looking briefly at what it is that makes each side in this impending negotiation interested in the other. If it is the Koreans who sought out and approached the Americans, then the latter should consider it a feather in their cap. Koreans research a prospective foreign partner with great care and thoughtfulness. In initiating contact they are paying you a substantial compliment on the quality of your company or organization. It means your ranking and reputation are very high; otherwise, they would not be interested. This does not necessarily imply, however, that their company is of equal quality. Check it out.

What Koreans are most interested in obtaining from their foreign partners are

- technology (to keep pace in their increasingly high-tech industries)

- prestige (from being associated with a world-class American company)

- increased export capability (and the hard currency this will bring in)

- profit (ultimately to flow especially from the public relations and marketing know-how of the American company and from the "pull" (see page 145) to be acquired by their connection with it)

The expectations of the American firm will differ somewhat:

- entry into the larger Asian market (a particularly strong motive)

- expansion of its share of the global market (a business relationship with this emergent economic powerhouse has its advantages)

- an easier place to begin in Asia than China and a less costly one than Japan (though a thorough understanding of the dynamics of the "post-economic-miracle" economy of Korea is essential—see chapter 13, pages 194–200 for an overview)

- profitability (early profits are a higher priority among the Americans than the Koreans, who are more interested in investing a larger share of the profits back into the enterprise)

Although no axioms for negotiating are fail-safe, there are a number of principles that will greatly enhance your probability of success if they are followed consistently.

Be prepared. The most common mistake made by American companies starting business negotiations in Korea is to think that they can "wing it," that they can reach an advantageous agreement simply by using their inherent skills and negotiating experience. When you add to this the general overconfidence Americans tend to display and their inclination to exaggerate claims and to brag about what they can bring to the deal (we have already made the point that these sorts of approaches are likely to be read by Koreans as "insincerity"—see chapter 6), you have a formula for failure and a surefire way of making certain your Korean counterparts will lose interest before you even realize what is happening.

In your prenegotiation planning, focus not only on determining what your company's desired outcomes are but on what those of your potential partner are as well. This will require a considerable amount of research about the target company before you even make contact with its representatives and certainly before you enter into negotiations. Then present your case from the perspective of its advantages to them, making the same points over and over again (skillfully), until you are certain the message has gotten through. In Korea sticking to your position and stating it repeatedly underscore your sincerity.

Make it clear that you don't expect and are not concerned with taking out quick profits. The Koreans will be more interested, as we have pointed out, in investing in the long-term development of a joint venture, which means that steady growth and the maintenance of good human relationships over the long term will be more important than short-term profits.

Instruct your negotiating team to be ready to discuss technical issues and other specifics in the most minute detail. The Korean negotiators will be sure to ask about them. This means including specialists on your team, first because they can provide technical data and information as needed (though they should not offer it until the U.S. team leader asks them to do so), and second because to the Koreans their presence will give a strong signal that you consider the negotiation a high priority and that you are sincere in your desire to reach an agreement and to begin a mutually beneficial relationship.

Prepare the members of your team to enter the negotiating room in the order of their rank (from top to bottom) rather than in the random order which informality-loving Americans prefer. Your team leader should be in obvious command and have the demonstrated respect of all the team members. The principal aims at the outset should be to give the best possible impression of your company and to lay the groundwork for developing a solid working relationship. Only then should you give attention to getting the best possible deal for your side.

Only the team leader should express the opinions and positions of the team. The negotiating room is not the forum for disagreements among your team members. Discuss differences of opinion in private caucuses. Nor should team members offer their technical or professional expertise until the team leader asks them to do so. When a team member wants to add essential information, he[†] should quietly pass a note to the leader and let him request the information.

Hire your own interpreter. Do not depend on using the Korean team's interpreter, who is, of course, on their side. Hire a professional who is experienced and skilled and brief him or her thoroughly before each session. Speak slowly and

---

[†] Korea is still, in the early twenty-first century, a male-dominated culture, as I've said before. Whatever you do, do *not* send a woman to represent your company. It would be absolutely foolhardy, and your politically correct action is likely to be interpreted as an insult by male executives.

distinctly and pause frequently to let the interpreter catch up. Use these pauses to gather your thoughts and to observe the body language and other reactions of those you are addressing. Be sensitive to the slightest signs indicating that the interpreter does not understand you. The English and Korean languages are polar opposites. Simultaneous translation is nearly impossible because verbs come at the end of the sentence in Korean and usually toward the beginning in English. The Korean language is often purposely vague and ambiguous, the meaning better sensed than articulated (remember the cultural trait of indirectness). Be ready to clarify what you mean and constantly check your interpretation of what the Koreans say.

Don't put all of your cards on the table early in the game. Succumbing to the American spirit of complete openness, which in many circumstances is admirable and productive, will cause you to lose the advantage or, even worse, to convey the wrong message when negotiating with Koreans. Always save some of your resources for concessions later.

Consider caucusing. Korean negotiating teams are not generally empowered to make decisions on the spot. Unlike Americans, the Koreans must caucus, consult their superiors, and reach agreement among themselves before making commitments at the negotiating table. You should also consider caucusing from time to time, if only as a tactic to emphasize the gravity of certain issues or to show that you are making unanticipated concessions (on-the-spot decisions may give the impression that you had planned all along to give in on a particular point).

Be prepared for the unexpected. The Korean team may bring up a point that was decided on earlier, just to see if what you say today is the same as what you said yesterday. More important, when sensitive, difficult issues arise, the Koreans may say something like "Let's sign the contract and settle this issue later." Don't do it. Insist on settling prickly issues *before* the contract is signed. I'll explain why in a moment.

Avoid using logic to back up your position. When you come to a clear point of disagreement, you will be tempted to explain the logic behind your position. However, because of the radical differences in thought patterns between Korean and American cultures (discussed in chapter 5), you can be sure your logical rationale will fall on deaf ears. A better strategy is simply to repeat your argument in greater detail, while explaining and emphasizing the advantages it has to the other side. Do this as patiently and as often as necessary. Repetition, as we have seen, is effective in demonstrating your sincerity and underscoring your key points to Koreans. In cases where your decision constitutes a more-or-less flat no, a fallback position is to suggest that headquarters or your superiors will not allow the requested concession.

At the end of each day, sum up orally what you consider major points of agreement reached and then follow up with a written summary circulated to both teams.

Maintain confidentiality—secrecy, if you wish—at all times. Confidentiality is extremely important but is sometimes difficult to achieve because the Korean grapevine is one of the most efficient in the world, and the other team will make every effort to gather as much intelligence as possible. This problem is aggravated by the fact that with disturbing frequency American negotiating teams end up with one or more members who believe that by ingratiating themselves with the Koreans and siding with them, they can bring the Korean team around to an agreement. Any clandestine effort to pursue such an aim is certain to undermine your team's bargaining power. Team members should be warned against taking such a step, and any members who do so should be sent home the moment such indiscretion is discovered.

Try to remove any team member or members who seems to cause a negative reaction among the Koreans. At some point, you may find one or more team members to whom the Koreans are reacting very negatively, for whatever reason. When you remove the person from the negotiating sessions, do so gently, if possible, by giving him outside assignments—until you've determined the significance of the negative reactions.

Be prepared to call in reinforcements. Many, if not most, negotiations reach an insurmountable impasse at some point. When that happens, you may need to call in help from whatever network of personal contacts you have in Korea—Koreans or Americans with long experience there. Ask them to intercede quietly and in whatever manner they judge to be most effective. This intercession will take place outside of the negotiating room, of course, principally in one-on-one meetings. You may also want to try changing the meeting place to help jar things loose, or you may actually bring to the negotiating table a mediator who understands both cultures thoroughly and who can act as an on-the-spot go-between to move the negotiations forward. If this proves to be effective, you should consider making that person a permanent member of your team.

Arrange informal meetings between the two team leaders at tearooms, coffeehouses, or bars during the negotiation process. This is one way to head off impasses and smooth the negotiating process in general. Even if the negotiations are not discussed, indeed especially if the negotiations are not discussed, these meetings can build good relationships between the team leaders and provide the two a forum for exploring *possible* breakthroughs when an impasse looms. *Possible* is emphasized here because neither of you can or should make commitments at informal meetings. This means a lot of tentative language such as "What if…?" "Is it likely…?" and "How would…?" but make sure it is clear that you are only exploring future possibilities, not making a concrete offer at that time.

Bring the American and Korean teams together outside the negotiating room. Shared social events serve an important function. The Koreans will probably take the initiative, but the American team should reciprocate. A banquet may help the teams through an impasse, and of course, a lavish one will be scheduled by each side after the contract has been signed. At these, and on other social occasions, the Americans would do well to let their hair down and show they are human, which is what the Koreans are likely to do.

At every opportunity emphasize that this venture will be part of a permanent, ongoing commitment. Reiterate as often as possible that the contract you expect to sign (or have signed) is only the beginning of a long and fruitful relationship. As for the contract itself, don't forget that traditionally Koreans have not thought it necessary to sign a piece of paper in entering a business venture with someone else. They do so today as a concession to Western conventions, though they can be assumed to know the implications of signing a contract. Nevertheless, be aware that they may view the same document from a different perspective.

From the Korean perspective, the negotiation process is more of a time to get to know the other party and to establish a good working relationship than to reach a paper agreement that is then expected to remain unchanged for the duration of the joint venture. In the past, Koreans entered contractual relationships through oral agreements based on a level of trust and faith sufficiently high to erase any doubts. This oral contract was considered binding—not for any predetermined and stated length of time but for as long as the personal relationship between the two parties exists. This is not so different from the traditional American method of making a deal, when a handshake sealed an agreement as solid as any contract.

Above all, remember that relationships between the parties are far more important than the contract. A corollary to this is that, for Koreans, commitments based on relationships can be much more binding than those on paper. Further, the Korean signer is likely to consider the contract to be applicable at the time of signing and only so long as all of the conditions remain exactly the same as they were at the point of signing, which, of course, they never do.

*Be advised that after signing the contract, your Korean coun-
terpart will continue to try to negotiate.* Usually this takes the
form of trying to get you to ease up on conditions to which
only their reluctant consent was given before signing. It does
no good to remind him that he has already agreed to that
condition and signed his name to it. Nor does it help to
explain yet one more time the Western logic which caused
you to insist upon the condition in the first place. And
finally, showing your anger at his bringing the matter up
again and again will certainly not help. These approaches
will only drive *you* crazy but will roll like water off your
counterpart's back. It is better to accept the likelihood that
he will continue to hound you on those points for the life of
the contract (or for your own lifetime, whichever is shorter!).
If you don't feel you can concede, give the Korean response
we've recommended elsewhere: suck in a long, audible breath
through your slightly parted lips and say, "Oh, it is very
difficult" as you slowly expel the air, and then repeat the
same statement every time the matter comes up—again and
again and again. Whatever you do, do not show the slightest
evidence that his constant requests are troubling to you, and
certainly don't give any signs that he is wearing you down.

Remember also that two can play that game. You are free
to pursue your partner with your own requests to revise certain agreements signed into the contract so they will be more
in your favor. This advice may be particularly useful when
the Koreans insist on sticking to clauses which are to *their*
advantage. In this light, take care to avoid incorporating into
the original contract unspecified options or ambiguous, open-
ended language.

It may strike the reader as strange that I have described the
Korean proclivity to keep the situation open as long as possible and, earlier in this chapter, to have simultaneously
urged you to bring every item to full and unambiguous closure
before signing the contract. This is not as contradictory as it
may seem. In the process of negotiation for a contract that

holds your own best interests to be of primary concern, keeping the situation open-ended as long as possible is advantageous. Nevertheless, before the contract is signed, you should do everything possible to nail down every minidetail in order to hold the other side to the exact agreement that has been hammered out.

****

Sometimes you fail in the end to come to an agreement no matter how hard and carefully—how sincerely—both sides have negotiated. In that case, try to leave behind positive feelings. Then, after a respectable period of silence, make contact again to see if the Koreans might be ready to change the positions that caused the breakdown, or if perhaps the circumstances that prevented agreement have changed. No, as will be no surprise to you by now, is rarely forever in Korea.

Managing a Korean Office

Attitudes toward working for a foreign company have changed considerably over the years. In the 1970s Koreans thought it desirable to work for Americans because the jobs carried clear benefits: higher wages, more training opportunities, faster and more individualized promotions, better working conditions, and occasionally, overseas travel.

Now, after more than half a century of exposure to the way American businesses operate abroad, Koreans tend to focus on the negative aspects of such a prospect. Lack of long-term job security is one. Foreign companies are much more likely than Korean companies to close their doors in Korea and return to their home countries, leaving their Korean employees out of work.* As Korea has grown more affluent, foreign firms have ceased paying top dollar. Promotions are more likely to come with greater regularity in Korean-owned firms, though recent legislation that makes it easier for employers to discharge their employees may be increasing the attractiveness of working for foreign companies—at least forcing Koreans to weigh more carefully the pros and cons of working

---

* Although the economic reversal of 1997–1998 did force many Korean companies to break the long-standing "social contract," before that time discharging permanent employees was unheard-of.

for one. Current economic conditions are also certain to have an effect on these issues.

Questions of permanence and prestige are central in making job choices. Some foreign companies are not first-rate, do poorly, and soon pack up and return home. Such companies often occupy rented facilities rather than a building of their own, and the signs that announce their presence are oftentimes made of flimsy, cheap materials. Koreans say that foreign-owned companies show less loyalty to their employees than do Korean companies. In American-managed companies, often the top positions are filled by imported and short-term managers, and these foreigners are, by definition, less familiar with and less sympathetic to Korean operating procedures, which causes morale problems within the office and leads to jokes and insults from fellow Koreans outside the office. Koreans who work for foreign firms are generally looked down upon by other Koreans.

Communication problems and cultural differences add to the difficulty, turning the best and the brightest potential job candidates toward Korean companies. Foreign firms are often reduced to raiding each other's top employees. This is especially the case in professions where there are not enough competent people to go around, such as scientists, technicians, and computer specialists.

This situation is being offset to some degree by the reversal of the brain drain that occurred earlier in the post-Korean War era. Now Koreans who go to the United States for graduate study, many of whom in earlier times remained in the U.S., are more likely to return to Korea to pursue their careers, increasing the supply of trained professionals with a working knowledge of English.

How does the typical American manager fare in Korea? Perhaps the best way to answer this question is to rephrase it: What do Koreans say when they bare their hearts and discuss what troubles or puzzles them most about their American partners?

Korean Complaints about American Bosses

One major concern is that the duration of the American manager's assignment in Korea is too short, usually two years, sometimes three. Most European multinational companies assign their key personnel to the same post for five to eight years. Seeing the constant change of personnel among Americans, the Koreans moan, "Just as Mr. Smith [say for example] was beginning to understand us and Korea and how things work here, they pulled him out and sent a new person who had to start all over again." They feel they are constantly breaking in new managers.

They note also that the arrival of Smith's replacement seldom allows for overlap, so there is no opportunity for Mr. Smith to introduce the new person to the Koreans with whom he will be working or to the broader network of important Korean contacts. If the overlap had been scheduled, it would have been possible for some of the trust built up over the years by the first manager to be transferred to the second. Mr. Smith's introducing him to the key Korean contacts would indicate that the new man can be trusted. Avoiding the overlap may be economical—sidestepping the seeming redundancy of having two high-priced managers unnecessarily in the same place at the same time—but it completely ignores the cost to the organization in rebuilding trust, reestablishing networks, and avoiding the inevitable blunders the new manager is certain to make.

Koreans also notice how often new managers immediately rearrange their office and make disruptive changes in routine procedures so as to "put their stamp" on them and obliterate anything which might remind anyone of the departed predecessor. If you must make changes, wait awhile first, then introduce them gradually, one at a time, and work hard at explaining them and making them stick. American managers don't realize that if a new practice fails, *they* suffer a damaging loss of face.

Koreans are appalled to hear new managers make negative comments about the person they replaced and even criticize the higher-ups in their own company or organization. As we have seen, Koreans tend to read such criticisms as insincerity. Why, they wonder, would anyone continue working for a company if it is so bad, or why would they not at least try to make such unfavorable comments less publicly?

They are also shocked at how many Americans outspokenly criticize Korean traditions and customs to their face, or within hearing range, and compare these traditions unfavorably with "superior" American customs. They cannot understand how American standards of politeness (or lack of such) permit them to say such things, even if, deep down, they truly feel that way.

Furthermore, Koreans are puzzled by how impatient Americans are. "Everything is a crisis for Americans, and everything should have been finished the day before it was begun." This impatience is reflected especially in the Americans' reaction to government regulations. Many newly installed American managers—with exaggerated confidence and more than a dollop of naivete—believe that with just a little extra effort, they'll have no trouble circumventing Korean red tape. But after trying scores of innovative schemes, they find that none work against the impervious Korean bureaucratic system, which steadfastly refuses to be circumvented. And, of course, none of this endears the offending Americans to the government officials, who will always have to be dealt with and who will always have the last word.

In the end, the most serious offender is American ethnocentricity. Too many Americans still take abroad with them the attitude that everything American is automatically better than everything in the host country. Not only is such an assumption unpleasant to observe and insulting to one's hosts, in Korea it blocks an avenue to winning the respect and goodwill of co-workers and acquaintances.

Korean Management Style

The importance of the Korean values of sincerity and a humble demeanor cannot be stressed enough, and Americans who demonstrate them have a major advantage in gaining the acceptance needed to function effectively. But what does "functioning effectively" in Korea mean? The basis for assigning people to overseas posts is generally their previous capability as managers at home. If American managers in Korea do everything that has always worked in the States, they will fail. U.S. management styles will not only not work in Korea, they will, in fact, be counterproductive.

For instance, what motivates Americans will not motivate the average Korean. Respect, status, title, face, recognition, seniority, and harmony in the workplace are more important than money or job satisfaction to Korean employees (see chapter 12 for more on the Korean worker). Just as foreigners in Korea must adapt to Korean cultural norms, so must they adapt to Korean organizational norms and modify their management style accordingly. This will not be a new concept to those familiar with *situational management*, in which one uses different styles to manage different types of employees. In Korea, however, once you have understood and mastered this basic style, there can be no variation. It must apply to relationships with all Korean employees. Let me explain.

Korean management style derives from the Confucian hierarchical structure of the society and is essentially authoritarian. It is closer to the kind of management commonly practiced in the United States fifty to seventy years ago than to the participatory management style prevailing today. For this reason Americans are likely to consider Korean management practices outdated or at least hopelessly old-fashioned. In fact, Korean management style is not so unusual among the world's cultures. It is carefully tuned to what one researcher calls a substantial power distance factor[†] in social

---

[†] See Geert Hofstede's *Culture's Consequences* (Beverly Hills: Sage, 1984).

and organizational relationships. *Power distance* is defined as the acceptance of inequality in rank, status, and authority, and it is evident in Korean organizations in the concentration of essentially unquestioned power and authority in "the boss." Americans who attempt to introduce more democratic, egalitarian, or participatory management methods find in most cases that these innovations not only fail to work, they actually create disruption, confusion, and discontent in the organization. And they may be seen as yet another sign of the American's "insincerity."

The management style practiced by most Korean executives and expected by most Korean employers is that of a benevolent dictator, with the emphasis, ideally, on benevolence, who is the embodiment of the values and virtues of the Confucian Gentleman Scholar or Superior Man. "Strong, decisive, patient, paternalistic, and involved" is the definition most often used for the successful and effective Korean boss.

In the scheme of things in Korea, underlings are most emphatically underlings. They are not supposed to disagree with their superiors, certainly not publicly. They do their job and provide information when it is requested. If they have good ideas for improving operations, they are expected to feed those ideas to their boss in private, allowing him to take credit for them and hoping he will remember to compensate or otherwise reward them later for having made the boss look good. A word of caution: maintain contact with subordinates only through the established channels of authority within the organization. Do not allow your employees to come to you to report on their supervisors or you will find yourself in endless trouble.

Another minor but important recommendation is to choose the most accurate translation into Korean of your job title and that of all of the Korean managers and supervisors you hire. These translations should not only be accurate, they should also be titles that in Korean give the greatest prestige to the bearer. Check this out carefully with bilingual Korean executives of your acquaintance or with Westerners with long experience in Korea.

As a manager in Korea, you will be forced to have much more contact with, and to accept control by, the bureaucracy than is necessary in the States. You will probably, if you are at all like the thousands of Americans who have preceded you, respond as if the Korean bureaucrats have no right to interfere as much as they do. This is not a healthy attitude to display in Korea. A little further on we will suggest a way to minimize your direct contact with the bureaucracy, but first let me say a few words on its behalf.

You need to remember that, in large part, it was Korean bureaucrats who devised the plans that laid the foundation for Korea's industrialization, including the creation of invest-ment capital and the needed infrastructure to make such phenomenal growth possible. They also set and maintained the priorities that achieved the most efficient utilization of their limited resources and that encouraged ever-increasing capital investment from abroad. While the economic col-lapse in 1997 cast shadows over this achievement, it never-theless caused Korea to become the Little Dragon most fully committed to the high-tech arena. So, while there undoubt-edly will be times when you wish to decry the Korean bureau-cracy, remember that it has had its benefits as well.

As should be more than clear by now, even with all the Western influences Korea has absorbed in the past century, it is still the most intact Confucian culture in Asia, which carries with it, as we have seen, the Confucian-based respect for the bureaucracy. One of the implications of this high regard is the fact that Koreans submit to government regula-tions and requirements in a much more accepting, less ques-tioning way than Americans do.

Not all Korean bureaucrats, however, have learned to re-ciprocate with a helpful, positive attitude and a willingness to serve the public, nor have they all learned to emulate the

Confucian Gentleman role now familiar to us. Instead, today, large numbers of bureaucrats are too ready to use their power to manipulate the system to their own advantage. By raising barriers to, rather than facilitating, the proper functioning of government, they assure their self-preservation, which (in many cases and crudely put) involves an increase in the size of the bribes they demand.

It is here, in the belly of the bureaucracy, that you are likely to run into examples of the Korean personality at its very worst. While 99 percent of all Koreans you will meet will match the description we have provided, that is, as the picture of humility and deference to others, it is in the bureaucracy that you will run into the exception and find the most officious, overbearing, and pompous people you have ever met. Now is the time to look as humble and nonthreatening as you can and to allow your senior Korean administrator to take charge while you remain silent. He will know how to act and what to say for maximum effectiveness.

For your part, when you are in the presence of such officials, try to show them as much deference and respect as your American self-assertiveness and innate sense of equality will permit. Dealing with the bureaucracy is likely to put you in the most uncomfortable situations you will be required to endure. Remember, always, that you and your company are going to be seeking favors from this pompous person in the future. Hang in there; be patient and persistent.

If you simply cannot abide dealing with difficult bureaucrats, the best advice is this: soon after your arrival in Korea, take your senior Korean administrator with you to pay a high-level courtesy call on all of the bureaucrats capable of affecting your business or professional affairs, and then leave all future contact in his capable hands. He will know the expected protocol and how to function effectively within its limits. He will know, too, how to develop good relationships with the working-level bureaucrats who have the ability to help move your case along by seeing that it is brought to the attention of the proper official—or to keep it from being sent to him! Despite the discouraging reality of the Korean bureaucracy, you can—if you work at it—establish good relations with many of the officials you encounter.

On many of the application forms you will be required to fill out when you want something, you will be asked to document why your petition should be granted. If you (either in person or through your Korean representative) have kept up good relations with the Korean officials, they will often tell you what reasons will give you the best chance of approval. In general, it is always a good idea to emphasize the benefits to Korea—through technological development, new jobs, expanded exports, and/or accrual of hard currency—your proposed actions will bring.

Because Korean career officials tend to be shifted from job to job with some frequency, you or your senior Korean administrator will need to make the rounds fairly often, establishing new contacts as needed. Keep track of any officials with whom you have good relationships. They frequently move within the same ministry and may be able to help you unexpectedly in the future. Good relationships can be maintained by going to these special friends among the bureaucrats from time to time to ask their opinion and advice, even on situations that are somewhat outside their domain. Koreans of all classes generally consider it a compliment if you ask them for their advice because doing so carries with it the implicit message that you consider that person to be the one who is knowledgeable and wise. You can always decide not to follow the suggestions if they are not useful.

Korean regulations are often insufficiently spelled out, open-ended, and unclear. One of your best sources of advice and help in these prickly matters will naturally be knowledgeable Koreans and other American expatriates, businesspeople, and professionals, the latter especially if they have had to navigate the same roadblocks you are facing.

Above all, the effective executive in Korea gives attention

to developing good human relationships within the office. The mutual trust that slowly and naturally results from such attention being paid to interpersonal considerations and to respecting other people's sense of human dignity and worth will be both striking and refreshing to the American who is a little jaded from the kind of long-term, obsessive concern with the bottom line that weighs so heavily in American executive offices. *Paternalistic* is perhaps an even better term than *benevolent dictator* for the proper attitude of a manager in Korea, where paternalism does not have the negative overtones it does in the United States. Indeed, Koreans have strong feelings of Confucian loyalty to their current employer and, for instance, proudly wear the company logo as a lapel pin. To see the organization as a kind of family, with the boss as paternal head, is both natural and comforting for them.

The more American managers can do to perpetuate and enhance the feeling of family in the Korean organization they run, the better chance they have of success. Take the custom of employees regularly eating and drinking together in local bars and restaurants after-hours. While following this practice often seems an imposition on Americans' private time, it serves a valuable function in the Korean organization, fostering congenial and supportive working relationships, enabling employees to give each other work-related feedback in a relaxed atmosphere, and allowing all staff members to let their hair down and blow off steam.

Other things you can do—which are not a normal part of one's role in managing an American company in the United States but do help foster relationships—are going to weddings or the "first 100-day" celebrations of your employees' children, attending school graduation ceremonies, or stopping at the hospital to visit an employee's wife.‡

---

‡ These experiences are rich in culture learning and valuable in themselves, but they will also further the aim of making the company seem more like a family to its Korean employees.

Two Key Relationships

There are two Koreans with whom you will want to establish a close and cordial relationship as quickly as possible. One is your Korean counterpart or partner, the chief or top manager of the Korean company with which your company has established a joint venture or other business, professional, or organizational relationship. The second is your senior Korean assistant.

As for the manager of your Korean counterpart company, concentrate on getting to know him as a person. In the process, you will come to identify certain aspects of his character and personality that you particularly admire. Does he, perhaps, meet the criteria of the classic Confucian Gentleman? Does he seem to have endless patience? Is he wise in an Asian way that opens to you different perspectives on life? Does he take particularly good care of his family? Whatever these key attributes are, let them serve as a channel to the deeper person and to special appreciation and respect for him.

In addition, identify areas of interest you share: Golf? Tennis? Hiking? Travel? Stamp or coin collecting? Invite him to attend sporting events with you. Take an interest in his family and in their individual achievements. Ask him to teach you about Korean culture (Appendix D provides a list of the various aspects of Korean culture you might ask him to explain). If he is interested in improving his English-speaking ability, perhaps you could offer to give him informal English conversation lessons in exchange for his teaching you Korean or about Korean culture. Be prepared to help him learn about American culture (Appendix E provides some relevant topics that might pique his interest). The efforts you make in this regard will be both rewarding and valuable in pursuing your shared business interests.

The second close and trusting relationship you need to establish is with your top Korean assistant. Since your senior

Korean administrator will become the most important person on your staff, it is necessary that he (and in Korea it will surely be a man) be selected with extreme care. If you select the right person and he does a good job, he will be worth whatever you have to pay him, no matter how much. There are so few qualified people available for this job that American companies often end up stealing the best of them away from each other. He will become not just your right-hand man but your whole right arm, with the absolutely essential job of integrating or weaving together the disparate American and Korean dimensions of your operations. The development of strong mutual trust between you is a sine qua non.

The senior Korean assistant's job description is like none you have read before. He is the person who oversees all operations on your behalf; he screens incoming information and communication; he "cuts through the smoke" and the confusion generated by the meeting of the two cultural worldviews; he interprets the language for you, but he also interprets the behaviors and intentions of the Koreans you deal with; he produces the right people when you need to hire someone; he helps you solve problems, correct situations, and repair damage when things have gone awry; he acts as your intermediary; he gathers information and researches issues critical to your operation. *He is indispensable.*

Here is a list of qualifications or descriptors for use in searching for this person. Some may seem strange at first, but if you weigh them in the context of what we have discussed so far about Korean culture and about the nature of Korean organizations, you will recognize the importance of each of these factors in narrowing down your choice to the right person:

- Native of the city your office is in (so he has the right connections and can easily find his way around)
- Respected ancestors (proper pedigree)

- Married (with at least one child)
- Graduate of a superior university
- Veteran of the Korean armed forces (preferably as an officer)
- Extensive contacts/network
- Substantial present occupation
- Good command of English
- Right salary level (including bonuses)

Your senior Korean administrator can also be of help in the case of conflict between you and your Korean counterpart, but he cannot be the mediator because he is, or should be, biased in your favor. He nevertheless must be kept up-to-date on the problem. You will need him solidly on your side. This need brings us back to the cautionary words written above: select your senior Korean administrator with the utmost care; you will have great need in this and in other sensitive matters to depend on his discretion and ability to keep a confidence.

When Disagreements Occur

Even with all of your best intentions and hard work at establishing a strong relationship, things will not always work out according to plan. The potential for disagreement and misunderstanding is high in any business or organizational relationship where two authority figures (you and your Korean counterpart) might vie for power. When the relationship involves two cultures as different as those we are concerned with here, the potential rises even higher. What do you do when that potential transforms into reality and a clash of wills, business interests, personality, or culture explodes into irrepressible conflict?

Actually there are several levels of intensity in most conflict situations, which may be charted as follows:

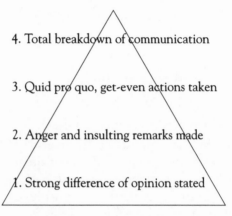

4. Total breakdown of communication

3. Quid pro quo, get-even actions taken

2. Anger and insulting remarks made

1. Strong difference of opinion stated

The action you take must be geared to the intensity level you're on at the time it becomes obvious that something needs to be done. There is a question prior to that, however, the answer to which needs to be clear in your mind. In what framework will you deal with the dispute? From which of the two cultural mindsets involved will it need to be approached? I hope there is no doubt as to the answer. Since the enterprise is in Korea and the person you are in conflict with is on his home turf, it is only reasonable to assume you will work out your differences within the operational expectations of the Korean human relations system.

If the clash is at the first level, you may not have a bona fide conflict situation at all. It may instead be more of a simple disagreement between two people who are in positions of leadership, at least in part because of their forceful personalities, but one through which two Confucian Gentlemen should be able to politely talk their way or at least reach a modus operandi which prevents an advance to the next level of intensity.

The best idea, obviously, is to catch things at the first level. Simply put, it means keeping your cool and restraining the inclination you might have toward assertiveness and confrontation and toward displays of emotion over having been wronged or at least frustrated in achieving a goal or winning an argument. In Korea, one thing most likely to call forth this kind of annoyed reaction in the American is, as described earlier, the persistent request for changes in the contract.

If the conflict has escalated to the second level, it is almost certain to require outside help in the form of a mediator or go-between. As we have seen, the use of go-betweens or mediators is common in Korea and does not imply the extremity of conflict it does in the United States. Anger and insult, while often fairly forgivable in an American setting, are a violation of accepted norms of Korean interpersonal behavior and sufficient cause for intercession. While at level 1 no one is likely to have irretrievably lost face, at level 2, and especially at levels 3 and 4, that risk becomes imminent and must be avoided at all costs if there is to be hope of maintaining effective operational relations.

In the event that mediation is called for, how do you choose a mediator? The critical qualifications are that the person be highly respected by both parties and be absolutely neutral. The mediator must also be as bicultural as possible. To be effective the mediator must be thoroughly grounded in both cultures and be able to understand and empathize with each at a relatively deep level. If an American, the mediator must have long experience in Korea with Koreans and be fluent in the Korean language; if a Korean, the same kind of experience is needed with Americans in the United States, along with fluency in English.

In Korea, *go-between* is actually the more accurate word to describe the role of the mediator, who will move patiently back and forth between the parties until a workable solution has been reached and who will probably never actually sit down with the parties facing each other to pursue mediation via direct communication. A good mediator will, however, follow up and maintain contact to assure that the achieved resolution remains in place.

There are, in addition, other actions to take and strategies to follow. One is to alert corporate headquarters as soon as it appears that the conflict will persist. It will not be easy for them to follow what is happening in any event, but their support, understanding, and empathy are needed to the degree they can be acquired.

Never speak to anyone against your Korean counterpart, even in the strictest confidence. (The exception is your Korean assistant, who will have to know about the dispute, but who must be absolutely trustworthy.) Also, think through and consider possible trade-offs you might offer ameliorate the situation.

Finally, in addition to protecting your counterpart's face, that is, making sure he is not overtly insulted or humiliated, be concerned about his kibun and the working relationship you share. Cultivate a sense of rightness and well-being between you. Keep the channels of communication open, and stress your belief that as two reasonable, civilized human beings you can maintain a respect for each other in spite of your differences. I recommended earlier that you put significant effort into developing a personal relationship with your counterpart. Now is the time to draw on it. A night out eating and drinking might be just the thing to get your shared respect for each other back in good working order.

If the deadlock is not broken after a reasonable period of time, replace the mediator. Once a successful resolution has been achieved, carry no grudges. Act as though there never was a problem between you.

It should be clear by now that it is the American partner who has the power to create conflicts or to prevent them, depending on his course of action and his ability to control himself. Confucius advised, "If a man would control his country, let him first control his family; and if he would control his family, let him first control himself; and if he would control himself, let him first control his heart."§

---

§ For East Asians, *heart* carries not only the idea of the emotional, empathetic, and compassionate meaning that it has for Westerners but also the thinking and reasoning implications that *mind* and *brain* have for Westerners.

12

Personnel Issues

Koreans make loyal, dependable, hardworking* employees. This results largely from Confucian feelings of extreme loyalty to one's group along with a desire for harmony and the acceptance of unequal status, all of which have their positive effects on management-labor relations, where management and labor consider themselves members of the same team. Working hard, however, is not in itself a Confucian virtue.

The other side of the coin is that this same impulse toward group loyalties, based on blood relationships, school ties, service in the same military unit, or in shared geographic origins, is so strong that it results in factionalism and the formation of cliques, which can be disruptive in the workplace. Recall, too, that nepotism is also endemic in Korea, more so than will be apparent at first.

---

* Americans who are familiar with Korean immigrants in the United States who work diligently in establishing small businesses in our cities sometimes refer to them as having a "Confucian work ethic." Because of its similarity to the "Puritan work ethic," it has an immediate appeal to Americans. But that term was concocted by American writers to make the phenomenon more comprehensible to Americans, and it is a misnomer. Confucius never recommended physical labor or "working hard." Indeed, the scholar-gentleman he promoted was not supposed to do any work at all!

The effective manager, as we saw in the last chapter, will attempt to channel this instinctive group bonding paternalistically into feelings of loyalty to the company or organization by emphasizing its similarity to a family and employing slogans, songs, logo pins, picnics, and so forth to build company spirit.

Hiring

Most Korean firms hire their future executives directly from the graduating class of Korea's universities. The top companies are able to attract the graduates of the best universities, with Seoul National University heading the list. Smaller companies have to be satisfied with taking their new hires from lesser institutions.

Graduating classes are hired in December at the end of the Korean academic year. Most companies give new hires at least a month of indoctrination in company policies and company spirit; this means that each year's crop of new managers begin work en masse in January. Class members retain their group identity and expect to be kept at more or less the same pay scale throughout most of their career (we will explain a little later the complex ways in which particularly talented employees receive additional compensation). During the first year the new hires will be rotated through most divisions of the company so they will become familiar with the whole range of its operations before more permanent assignments are made.

Since university graduates are the traditional source of all incoming managerial personnel, the normal processes familiar to American corporations, such as recruiting, interviewing, selecting, and hiring, are not carried out on an individual basis throughout the year but rather as a group activity once a year. Also, since the hiring procedure will be carried out in Korean, you, as an American manager or executive, will be less involved in these procedures than you might assume. Except for a ceremonial welcoming speech, which will be quite general and inspirational in tone, everything will be handled by your senior Korean administrator and other Korean officers, as appropriate.

A second source of employees is referrals from people in your Korean network, once you have developed it, and recommendations from the top people in your organization; these incoming employees may be handled on an individual rather than a group basis. Care should be taken in hiring by referral or recommendation so as not to aggravate the problems of nepotism and factionalism mentioned earlier. Make a conscious effort to limit the number of employees of any one ingroup to maintain a balance. Newspaper ads are used less frequently in Korea than in the United States, especially for filling higher-level jobs. Search firms were established in the 1980s for finding top executives, and this, in addition to hiring the crop of new university graduates, seems to be the direction of the future. Clerks, accountants, and secretaries are frequently hired through ads, however.

What types of jobs are you going to find Koreans best suited for? Knowing this will help you decide when it is safe to vest responsibility early on and when you may want to supervise more closely. Here are some areas where Koreans are likely to be especially strong performers (primarily because they understand the Korean character intuitively):

- public relations
- customer relations and customer service
- liaison for networks of Korean contacts (at all levels and throughout the country)
- liaison with the Korean bureaucracy
- labor relations
- marketing

182

Termination

If hiring is a difficult process, letting someone go is even more so, especially if done according to accepted Korean practices. Even if you follow the guidelines discussed below when dealing with an unsatisfactory employee, you may still have to terminate someone, but you will at least be able to say that you did everything possible to give him or her a second (or third or fourth) chance. You will have demonstrated your sincerity and your understanding of the people orientation of Korean culture and the need to do everything possible to avoid making someone lose face. In addition you will make your other employees feel more secure in knowing that they too are not likely to be fired in a frivolous manner and that their American boss is a humane, caring person who understands how traumatic such an event is for the employee's entire family.

If, in the end, discharge is necessary, the person will still get a generous separation payment often accompanied by a face-saving framed citation noting the person's faithful years of service to the company. Disingenuous or hypocritical, Americans might say, but in Korea such gestures are a genuine display of sincerity.

Clearly, dealing in the Korean manner with an unsatisfactory employee will require a great deal of your time and attention and will involve you on a much more emotional and personal level than would be necessary in the United States. This much must be said for the Korean system, however: in all my years as a manager in Korea, it was only necessary for me to take the drastic step of firing someone once.

Should you need to initiate this long and complicated process leading toward possible dismissal, the first thing to do is to turn the job of communication of an initial reprimand over to your senior Korean administrator to handle privately. Only when this has failed after successive attempts should you as manager step into the process. In your first private meeting with the person, you should convey—by both words and actions—how terribly reluctant and embarrassed you are to bring this matter up, but that the situation has finally forced you to intervene. Beyond that, you should be more generic than specific in naming the particular complaints you have against the person. Refer to them, but only in a vague and unspecified way. At this point, your aim is still to reform rather than to discharge.

At the second meeting, if one is necessary, become more specific. By the third meeting, you should provide the employee with a detailed written list of his or her wrongdoings as well as a specific recital of what the next step—termination—will be if the employee does not improve. Before the end of the meeting, set a date for the next appointment, in which you will evaluate any progress. During these meetings also continue to emphasize how very difficult it is for you to consider the ultimate action, but that without improvement you will have no alternative.

Meanwhile, your senior Korean administrator will have begun to keep a file of information specifying the employee's offenses. He should also, according to established Korean custom, collect a handwritten letter from the employee, signed with his or her personal seal, in which the individual recognizes his or her wrongdoings, asks for forgiveness, and promises never to commit them again. Your senior Korean administrator will see to it that the employee continues to rewrite the letter until it is accurate and sufficient in every detail.

Other actions—short of dismissal—can be taken to reinforce the message. One is to reassign the employee to a less central location, possibly more than once, making each successive assignment less appealing. Another step is to demote the person, deny regular promotion, change the employee's status from full-time to part-time, or in the extreme, reassign the individual to a newly created job with a low-level title, smaller office, and no work to do.

While you have avoided causing a major loss of face all at once, the employee's face is nevertheless coming apart piece by piece. It is likely, therefore, that he or she will decide to leave the company voluntarily. To an American this may appear to be a bizarre way to deal with an unsatisfactory employee; to Koreans it is not.

Other Personnel Issues

Effective management requires a set of company rules and regulations. These will likely have been carefully developed previously by a task force of top Korean managers and have been well publicized throughout the company. At the time of employment, it is customary for incoming employees to sign a statement indicating that they have read and understand company rules and policies and willingly agree to them. These rules should, among other things, clearly stipulate that poor performance, absence without notification, insubordination, or misdemeanors of any kind are cause for the taking of certain specified actions. These can include such things as a letter of apology from the offending employee (as in the procedure outlined above), the issuance of a written warning, or certain specific disciplinary actions. It is customary in such documents to indicate that three such letters in the employee's file describing separate incidents are cause for dismissal. These policies are used for blue-collar and white-collar workers up to midlevel management, but not for upper-level management.

When the employee who has violated the rules complies and improves in performance, the punitive actions are quickly abandoned, the employee's status reinforced with a good assignment, and no further action is taken. Things proceed as if nothing improper ever happened.

Compensation. Korean compensation practices are in some ways so different from American practices as to arouse the suspicion of a newly arrived American manager. We will want, therefore, to examine them with some care.

There are three distinct parts to compensation in Korea: the base salary, variable allowances that are added to that base pay for specific purposes, and some companies pay four extra months' salary as bonuses. This practice is in the process of changing. At least 25 to 30 percent of the companies have now abandoned the practice of paying separate bonuses and have simply included that money in the regular salary. The base pay is determined by the employee's seniority or length of time with the company. All of the people with comparable education and at comparable job levels who came into the company at the same time—on graduation from either university or high school—will receive the same base pay. This portion of their compensation is much more standardized than in the United States, with the Korean government setting the guidelines as to what this base amount should be.[†] Companies are expected to make their base pay schedule public and to distribute it among their employees.

The allowances portion of the salary, on the other hand, varies greatly among employees and is often used to acknowledge and reward diligence and high-quality performance; it can increase an employee's base pay as much as 100 percent. These additions have various names: position allowances, family allowances, or allowances to cover housing, transportation, overtime, professional licenses, research, and English-language training. Categories become blurred in order for a manager to reward those who genuinely deserve to receive higher pay. A supervisor, for example, might increase an employee's transportation allowance to reward loyalty and hard work, whether he or she has transportation costs or not. Annual cost-of-living adjustments are made as needed.

In keeping with the Korean attempt to maintain a paternalistic atmosphere in their organizations, considerable "psychic pay" is added to the salaries of Korean workers each

---

[†] Companies accomplish this by setting their rates to correspond to those of government employees.

month. These psychic rewards include everything from office wide picnics to wedding gifts to attendance at funerals and/ or other special personal events. Some companies give scholarships to pay for the schooling of their employees' children. Some lend interest-free "key money"‡ to assist their employees in meeting housing expenses.

Selected top managers may be provided with a company car and/or access to confidential funds to cover entertainment expenses for company clients. No receipts are required to prove that these funds were actually spent for entertainment.

There are no pension plans to provide for ongoing retirement; instead, it is customary for Korean companies to pay a fairly large lump-sum separation payment when the employee retires. The amount of this payment is set by government regulation at one-twelfth of the employee's annual salary times the number of years worked.

Training. As recently as 1990 training in Korea was considered essentially a means of learning or upgrading manual and/ or technical skills. Since then up-to-date management training from the United States has become a fad. Korean chaebŏls, such as the giant Samsung Corporation, have erected multimillion-dollar training campuses on the outskirts of Seoul, and there is a frenzied effort to bring in the author of the latest pop American best-seller on management theory and to launch executive training programs in modern American management techniques. All of this may seduce one into thinking that training programs developed in the U.S. for American trainees are equally well suited for the Korean

---

‡ "Key money" refers to a large sum of money paid to landlords instead of monthly rent and amounting to several thousand—sometimes tens of thousands—of dollars, which the renter puts up as an interest-free loan at the beginning of the rental period. The landlord invests this money in lieu of rent during the time the tenant is living on the property. The money (that is, the principal) is returned when the renter moves out. It is a common practice in Korea.

management environment. They are not, but it will take some time for Koreans to discover this fact and for the fad to run its course. Only then will it be possible to develop training programs that are a closer fit to Korean cultural patterns and thought processes.

In dealing with training needs, the American manager should be alert to issues arising in three areas: (1) Korean perspectives on learning, (2) trainer behavior, and (3) effective training styles and techniques. First, a word of caution. In Korea an assignment to training is sometimes considered a thinly veiled criticism of the employee's performance. This is not a major issue, but a pep talk, especially for older staff, reassuring them of their importance and the value of the training, will be useful in allaying this concern.

Korean Perspectives on Learning. Traditionally, Korean education is based on rote learning and, as we have seen, on thought processes that are much more nonlinear than linear. Education is also more oriented toward deductive than inductive reasoning. Experiential learning styles and the American orientation toward innovation, if allowed to dominate the training process in undiluted form, are likely to produce more confusion than motivation to learn among tradition-bound Koreans. It can be expected to work more successfully with younger Koreans, particularly if they have received some of their education in Britain or the United States.

Trainer Behavior. The single most important thing for trainers to understand is that they will be perceived by the Korean trainees as experts. Recall the attitude of respect and reverence paid to teachers described earlier. This attitude carries over to trainers and includes the expectation that the trainer is all-knowing and will be able to answer any question put to him or her. Failing to do so—which is perfectly acceptable in the American educational context—will mean a significant loss of face and is to be avoided.

Trainers should maintain an essentially formal relationship with the trainees, resisting their egalitarian impulses toward informality to reduce the risk of losing the trainees' respect. It also calls for formal attire and a general demeanor that communicates authority. Since many American trainers have made the mistake of sitting on the table, I must also advise you against this rather typical American behavior.

Training Styles and Techniques. Here are guidelines that will greatly enhance the effectiveness of your training:

1. Adapt training styles to Korean learning expectations.

2. Depend heavily on lectures or lecture/demonstrations, especially at the beginning.

3. Simplify the steps to be taken in a program and organize and present them clearly, so that the trainees are fully aware of and understand the rationale for their progression from point to point. The separation between each step needs to be sharply demarcated.

4. Avoid presenting trainees with too many choices or options in the early stages—this tends to produce more confusion than learning.

5. Shake the habit, ingrained in Americans, of ending the presentation of a point with "Now, are there any questions?" There is little likelihood of a response (except perhaps from someone familiar with Western education who wishes to please the trainer) and a high probability of embarrassment. Most trainees will be reluctant to ask questions in front of their peers, which from their perspective would expose their own ignorance or, worse, imply publicly that the trainer has done an inadequate job of presenting the material. A better approach would be to break the trainees into small groups of three or four and ask them to formulate one or two questions that would help illuminate the subject under consideration. Then, back in the whole group, the trainer can provide answers to those questions.

6. Hold off on the use of experiential learning activities, such as role plays and simulations, until the trainees are comfortable with the trainer, the program, and each other. The embarrassment potential will be great if the trainer introduces these too early. Such activities will be most effective if used at the end of a carefully designed sequence that moves them step-by-step toward focusing on applications (in case studies, for instance) and increasing participation in the learning process. Figure 1 below presents a model of such a progressive design.

7. As soon as the training session is over, prepare an accompanying lesson summary sheet that addresses, in simple outline format, everything that has been covered in the workshop, in the same sequence it was presented in the training sessions, and with each step clearly numbered. Korean trainees are generally willing to spend long hours mastering the content. It also gives them a resource for future reference.

8. Recognize the participants' successful completion of the program with impressive certificates awarded at an impressive ceremony and, if possible, with salary increases or some other financial reward.

One way of dealing with the needs of the Korean trainees is to follow what I call the Progression Model in helping them make the transition from the deductive to the inductive approach or, put another way, from the lecture/didactic to the experiential mode. The succession of methodologies looks something like this:

Figure 1: Progression Model

1. Lectures

2. Lectures plus Q-and-A Sessions
   (with the questions to be developed in small
   groups as described above)

3. Whole-Group Discussions

4. Small-Group Discussions
   (in groups of three or four and with a
   representative chosen to record the points made
   and to report back to the full group)

5. Discussion Based on Agree-Disagree Statements
   (with small groups assigned the task of coming to
   consensus; the groups should be allowed to change
   the statements if they wish so that all members
   personally agree with the statements)

6. Single-Solution (programmed) Case Studies

7. Multiple-Solution Case Studies
   (emphasizing multiple acceptable solutions rather
   than one "right" one)

8. Role Plays
   (starting with nonthreatening scenarios and
   moving to increasingly riskier ones)

This model calls for trainer support and encouragement of
the trainees as they progress toward the increased risk taking
and greater involvement required by the evolving training
style. It therefore demands a relatively long training program
rather than the one- or two-day program frequently used and
found effective with groups of Americans.

There is another approach to this problem, which I refer to
as the Adaptation Model. It involves identifying one Korean
or a small working group of Koreans, ideally bicultural and
thoroughly familiar with both traditional didactic and expe-

riential training methods, who can work closely with the American trainer (or with American off-the-shelf training programs) in adapting the highly experiential American training techniques to the Korean audience.

Challenges Facing Korea

Both North and South Korea recently came into prominence in world news in three rather dramatic ways:

1. The sudden economic collapse, in late 1997 and 1998, of several East and Southeast Asian countries. Although it actually began in Thailand and Malaysia, the full impact of this catastrophe was first felt most completely in South Korea. As of this writing, Korea has largely recovered, but long-term measures to ensure future economic health have not yet been put in place.

2. The worsening of the effects of three consecutive years of devastating droughts and floods in North Korea (1995–1997). This country had succeeded up to that point in hiding most of the details of its true conditions from the outside world, until it, too, reached the point of imminent economic collapse, long before South Korea's economic setback.

3. The surprise agreement in mid-2000 between North and South Korea that allowed their heads of state to meet in a friendly manner for the first time since partition of the country in 1945.

North Korea's current situation is, in many ways, even more alarming, so far as the future economic recovery of South

Korea is concerned, than anything going on within South Korea could possibly be. If the South were suddenly required to assume the full responsibility for bailing out the North as well, this would clearly present far more of a problem than the rigid requirements of the repayment of what was, up to that point, the largest loan in the history of the International Monetary Fund (IMF), made in an all-out attempt to bring economic recovery to South Korea.*

Although this book is mainly focused on the cultural aspects of the Korean people, the implications of the first two items above can hardly go unnoticed or unmentioned by anyone writing a book on Korea today. The credibility of any author who would produce a book on the country while seemingly being totally unaware of these calamities would certainly be stretched beyond believability, because the issues will have an enormous effect on Korea for years and even decades to come. On the other hand, neither of these situations changes the subject matter contained in this book: the values, assumptions, and thought processes of the Korean people.

The 1997 Economic Collapse

South Korea was the first country in Asia, other than Japan (which had a hundred-year head start on all the other Asian countries in modernizing), to follow what has come to be known as the "Japan Model" for development. By making Japan's economic success the model for its own, South Korea was able to raise its own economy from the status of an "underdeveloped nation" as late as 1960 to become a "fully developed nation" a mere thirty to thirty-five years later, as the invitation to membership into the Organization for Economic Cooperation and Development in 1996 indicated. By

---

* At the time of this writing, the IMF crisis is over, but it caused much internal turmoil, earlier, in South Korea.

early 1997 tiny South Korea had also become the eleventh largest economy in the world.

The Japan Model is the only model that has proved itself to be successful in transforming a Third-World nation into a First-World power, and South Korea has the distinction of being the first country ever to make that full transition, thus providing evidence for the effectiveness of the model. The Japan Model can make this miraculous change possible even for nations that, like Japan and South Korea, have virtually no raw materials and no oil for their energy source.

The formula for the Japan Model can be spelled out most simply as follows:

- Importation of 100 percent of the country's raw materials.

- Importation of 100 percent of the oil necessary for the country's source of energy.

- Full government support and planning for the country's economic development.

- Manufacture of increasingly more complex and expensive products of high quality.†

- The sale of these products to an ever-expanding *world* market.

In the second phase the government must do whatever it takes to climb as close to the top of the world economic chart as humanly possible by

- keeping the hourly wage rate as low as possible for as many years as it can (South Korea managed to hold down its labor cost longer than any other Asian country),

---

† South Korea's exports to the world market, believe it or not, began with paper and silk flowers and then progressed, in rapid succession, to hand-knit wool sweaters, wigs, leather shoes, and then to simple kitchen appliances, next to more complex electrical products, and finally to electronic products and automobiles.

- providing a structure that facilitates long-range planning (for twenty years or more), then sticking to that plan, regardless of who becomes president or prime minister,

- determining which products will be produced and by which companies, concentrating on the largest conglomerates (in Japan, the *Keiretsu*; and in Korea, the chaeböl) and favoring them in every way,

- producing all of the funding for research and development for the products it has chosen to concentrate on, and then providing all of the resulting information to the favored recipients free of charge,

- passing protectionist laws and restrictions and high tariffs on imports to protect sales within its own country,

- encouraging its citizens to save as much money as they can, live as frugally as possible, and, initially, buy only products produced locally,

- making it easy for the chosen companies to borrow as much money as needed (at artificially low interest rates) to expand their production to the greatest extent possible,

- covering companies' loans when needed so they will not go bankrupt and repaying the banks to cover any bad loans (cronyism and favoritism have often been involved in the piling up of bad investments and loans in Korea and in all of the other Asian countries except Singapore),

- taking other countries' popular inventions and intellectual properties and reproducing them freely and selling them for less than the originating country is able to do, and

- selling its products for less than it costs to manufacture them (a practice known as "dumping") in order to convince other countries to start buying from it rather than its competitors (also resorting to bribes and pay-offs as necessary, to achieve the same effect).

Western economists knew for some time that without change and correction, there would eventually be a time limit to the workability of the Japanese Model. We now know that limit is thirty to thirty-five years. But the model was extremely successful while it lasted. And for a while it looked like it might even last forever, because the government of each country using the model carefully controlled all aspects of its success for its own benefit, often pouring good money into failing projects and covering up for them. Certainly the citizens of all of the Asian countries expected their "miraculous" success formula to go on forever. When the formula began to fail and the economies of the countries began to collapse in late 1997, the people then blamed their political leaders for having done something wrong, rather than realizing that the formula itself had a built-in time limit before it was bound to self-destruct in an economy that has become a world economy.

Japan began its present recession in 1991. Japan knew precisely what steps it must take to make the changes necessary to correct its ailing system. All of the changes related to reducing government control and manipulation, converting to a competitive world market system, and totally restructuring its banking system to eliminate cronyism by avoiding inappropriate loans and the covering up of government repayment of bad loans. Yet Japan has failed to make the changes it knows are necessary because the changes are not easy, and they will not have a quick payoff. There are no quick fixes. The changes that are absolutely necessary will require the government to ask its citizens to suffer for perhaps five or ten years before the economy is eventually restored. How can anyone expect sane politicians to put into effect measures that will guarantee they will not be reelected?

The economic systems of all of Asia's original Four Little Dragons (or Four Little Tigers)—South Korea, Taiwan, Hong Kong and Singapore—as well as the Three New Little Dragons (Malaysia, Indonesia and Thailand) must eventually be brought to a similar correction over the same difficult five- to ten-year period of reform. There are no easy fixes for them either.

It is my firm belief that South Korea, however, because of its past record and achievements, has the best chance of all of the fifteen countries on the Asian side of the Pacific Rim of tightening its belt and setting into place the measures it knows are a prerequisite to making its economy well again. South Korea's president, Kim Dae Jung, as he began his term of office, gave every indication he would make the hard (and unpopular) changes that, slowly but surely, would revive Korea's lagging economy. It was impossible for him to keep his program on track, however, as the people began to resist the painful measures he began in good faith to install. Success in this effort is by no means assured, and the current revival of Korea's economy should be seen as only a short-term correction, with much restructuring to be undertaken before its recovery will be firmly rooted.

In the mid-1980s South Korea's major industries were steel, shipbuilding, automobiles, computers, and electronics. These were exactly the same specializations that Japan was emphasizing at the same time. It was clear to every observer that Korea had set its sights on catching and eventually surpassing Japan. At that moment, however, South Korea could not even make all of the component parts to supply its own automobile and computer manufacturing companies and was forced to purchase several high-tech components from Japan. Japan's high-tech expertise was far ahead of South Korea's. Yet, because Japan's wages were higher, Korea could under-price Japan for its finished products and then sell them to Eastern Europe, Latin America, and China, where cost was more of a determinant in purchasing decisions than quality or service. So, in the short run, Korea was still competitive.

At the same time Korea realized that it was a long way from obtaining its ultimate goal and that as long as it maintained the status quo, it would become less and less competitive with every passing year. In 1992 South Korea, under President Kim Young Sam, made some hard decisions. Although the country had not yet caught up with Japan, he announced that Korea would join the high-tech world leaders (such as the United States and Japan) by the end of the century, and the end of the century was at that time only eight short years away! This was a major decision, and one that would be even harder to achieve than South Korea's original economic miracle, which began in 1965. He named this ambitious campaign "Operation G-7." Its goal was to put itself on a par with the G-7 nations, the world's most advanced countries.

It should be pointed out that South Korea's decision was radically different from a decision taken by one of the other Little Dragons, Taiwan. At that moment, Taiwan was deciding instead to try to maintain its competitive advantage by continuing at its present level of technology and by making an effort to expand its customer base. In addition, Taiwan decided to allocate more than three hundred billion U.S. dollars for completely redoing the country's infrastructure (in order to make it more attractive to foreign investors).

The point is that Korea did not shy away from making the hard choice, and Taiwan did. South Korea realized that if it could not compete technologically, it would begin dropping further and further behind. It really had no choice, so it decided on several areas of technology to develop, specifying such advanced areas as

high-definition television	fiber optics
semiconductors and memory chips	nuclear energy
	CD-ROM drives
electric vehicles	satellites
robotics	

Next the government selected which companies to give government grants to for the development of the capabilities necessary to gain the skills in these designated areas. By 1994 South Korea had begun to manufacture flat-panel computer screens, had entered the computer memory chip industry, and had via Samsung become the world's largest supplier of dynamic random access memory chips, producing one quarter of the chips for the entire world market. By 1995 South Korea was making active-matrix liquid crystal display screens (for advanced color notebook computers and for portable televisions). Also by 1995, South Korea, France, and Japan had become the three top developers of civilian nuclear energy for the world market. South Korea once again proved that it can gear itself up to achieve the impossible.

Korea was not happy to accept the strict stipulations that the IMF imposed before approving the huge loan to help Korea climb out of the economic collapse that came in late 1997, yet it had no choice. It was those very requirements (as well as additional ones being made by the World Trade Organization, plus the demands that the U.S. trade negotiators have been attempting to impose upon Japan, without success, for the past several years to force Japan to "level its playing field") that Japan, South Korea, and all of the other Asian countries will ultimately have to meet before they can revitalize their lagging economies. This will not be easy, nor will it come quickly.

The Imminent Collapse of North Korea

The only thing that South Korea needs to fear (besides the five or ten years of suffering it must go through) is that North Korea might collapse during this time of restructuring, leaving South Korea to pick up the entire tab, not only for its own complete recovery from the 1997 recession but also for North Korea's failed economy at the same time. In past years many South Koreans have yearned for the day when their divided country might be made whole again, but this is not the time South Korea can take on the rebuilding of both halves simultaneously.

The case of the two Germanys comes to mind, although these two cases are nowhere close to being similar in scale. West Germany's economy was far larger and healthier than South Korea's (before the collapse of its economy). When East Germany fell, its per capita income was one quarter of that of West Germany's, while North Korea's is one eighth (or less) of that of South Korea's. Also, there were four times as many West Germans as East Germans, while there are only twice as many South Koreans as North Koreans. Besides, South Korea's GNP is only one fifth of West Germany's at the time of the reunification of the two Germanys. So the comparison only goes to prove how much more difficult it will be for South Korea to take on the responsibility for reunification than it was for West Germany to join the two halves of that divided country.

Estimates were that it would have taken close to one trillion U.S. dollars plus an entire decade for South Korea to rehabilitate North Korea—that is, if the late 1997 economic collapse had not occurred. South Korea has now shifted its hopes and plans to look forward to the reunion of the two Koreas by the year 2020 at the earliest. The big question now is, of course, whether they or anyone else can hold off the inevitable collapse of North Korea to conveniently fit South Korea's timetable.

North Korea fears that an immediate reunification would mean that South Korea would simply swallow the North—in the manner in which West Germany swallowed East Germany—literally causing North Korea to disappear without so much as a trace remaining of all the suffering the country had gone through this past half-century.

I am indebted to Korean scholar Bruce Cumings for convincing me that the prospects for the eventual reunification of the two Koreas now look quite hopeful. As he has pointed out, this optimistic expectation grows out of three preconditions:

1. The staying power of North Korea—which did not, like its mentor state, the Soviet Union, collapse—in spite of the repeated famines caused by drought-produced crop failures in 1995–1997.

2. The enlightened understanding and the public statement of South Korean president Kim Dae Jung that he does not have a "German policy" toward the North for absorbing North Korea into South Korea, thereby causing it and its political ideals of the last half-century to disappear forever. Rather, he conceives of the North's continuing as a "federated autonomous region" for as long as it needs (Cumings estimates this to take twenty or thirty years) but in a close relationship with the Southern federated autonomous region.

3. The recognition in 1997 by North Korea's leader, Kim Jong Il, that a strong and continuing American presence is necessary in the region because, for the first time in history, both China and Japan are equally strong at the same time. The U.S. presence can deter either of these Asian giants from repeating the threats to Korea's independence that made Korea the pawn of China, Japan, and Russia a century ago.

Having pointed out the catastrophic situations that confront Korea during the beginning years of the new millennium, I want to voice my confidence in the indomitable spirit of the Korean people, who have faced difficult periods multiple times in their past and who will, I am certain, rise again to become a dominant Asian and even a major world power. As mentioned earlier, in 1994 the *Economist* projected that South Korea will become the world's seventh largest economy by the year 2020. I believe that the Koreans will still be able to meet this goal, despite the setbacks they have faced.

Afterword

I started this book with the observation that in 1940 virtually no one in the United States knew what or where Korea was. That is remarkable enough. But what is almost more amazing is that even today, in spite of the Korean War and South Korea's economic miracle as well as its more recent economic collapse, and despite the surprising and promising efforts in the year 2000 of North and South Korea to begin planning their ultimate reunification, there is still amazingly little known about Korea.

Much of the blame for this ignorance must be credited to the effective isolation which for many centuries Korea, as the Hermit Kingdom, imposed on itself. A considerable amount must go also to academic historians who, well into the twentieth century, considered Korea to be only a provincial outpost of China. Korea did borrow much of the base of its civilization from its giant neighbor, but then so did Japan, and Korea's culture is as different from China's as Japan's is from China's.

This widespread ignorance about Korea has a couple of implications for those with a personal stake in learning as much as they can about the country. In the first place, it means there is much to explore by whatever means, in whatever places, using all of the sources this rich culture offers. Secondly, it will be difficult to find much information from the limited literature available. Therefore, I have included a number of information-laden appendices along with a select but substantial bibliography to help.

My final suggestion, as I near the end of this book, is to ask readers to recall some of the most important points they have learned during the reading to help them to "think Korean." To assist, I am going to close with a few points I hope have been learned from this book.

1. *Prepare yourself to be considered a foreigner throughout your stay in South Korea.* As a foreigner, you will never be allowed to enter Korean society fully and completely. This point may seem obvious, but the contrast with life in the United States is so striking, it is significant. In the States we have an attitude that as soon as foreigners arrive, they should give up their foreign ways and start doing things the way we do them. Perhaps we force Americanization on them too soon, but at least we don't hold them back from becoming Americans the way Koreans hold foreigners back from being thought of as Koreans.

2. *Whenever you need to meet a Korean, you can't just give a quick phone call, introduce yourself, and set up an appointment.* Instead, you have to find someone who knows you and the person you want to meet and ask that person to introduce you.

3. *Life in South Korea is far more formal than in the United States.* Ritual and protocol are terribly important. It is especially important that you observe and master the simple rituals of daily life as quickly as possible.

4. *Learn to live with ambiguity in South Korea.* You never know precisely what is going on at any time. Aside from the language barrier, Koreans operate with what I call

"polite inexplicitness." They intentionally remain vague, trying to remain open and undecided as long as possible. And not wanting to disagree with you, they will often say yes when, in fact, they mean no. After a time, though, you will be able to ascertain their true meaning—most of the time.

****

Happy exploring; you're in for the adventure of your life!

Appendix A

Korean Chronology

Human habitation from about 600,000 years ago, but most activity from 30,000–6000 B.C.	PALEOLITHIC PERIOD
From ca. 6000–1000 B.C.	NEOLITHIC PERIOD
2333 B.C.	Mythical founding of Korea by Tan'gun
ca. 1000 B.C. to 300 B.C.	BRONZE AGE
ca. 300 B.C.– 1 B.C.	IRON AGE
108 B.C.–A.D. 313	Chinese settlement of Lolang (Korean: Nangnang) established in Pyŏngyang area
57 B.C.–A.D. 668	THREE KINGDOMS PERIOD: (beginning of historic period)
37 B.C.*–A.D. 668	KOGURYŎ KINGDOM
18 B.C.†–A.D. 660/663	PAEKJE KINGDOM
57 B.C.‡–A.D. 668	OLD SHILLA KINGDOM
A.D. 42–A.D. 562	KAYA FEDERATION§

---

* Traditional date but probably more accurately first century A.D.; Koguryŏ
† Traditional date but probably more accurately ca. A.D. 250; often spelled "Paekche."
‡ Traditional date but probably more accurately ca. A.D. 300; often spelled "Silla," but always pronounced "Shilla."
§ Actually four kingdoms, but because Kaya was aligned with Japan, it is often ignored.

208

372	Buddhism introduced into Koguryŏ Kingdom from China
552	Chinese culture transmitted to Japan via Korean Paekje Kingdom
668-935	UNITED SHILLA PERIOD
918/935–1392	KORYŎ DYNASTY
1231, 1274, 1281	Mongol invasions
1234	Invention of movable metal type in printing
1237–1252	Carving and printing of major Buddhist text, Tripitaka Koreana (from 81,258 wooden blocks) ‖
1260–1895	Korea under suzerainty of China during most of Yuan, Ming, and Ch'ing (Qing) Dynasties
1392–1910	CHOSŎN (YI) DYNASTY
1446	Development of phonetic Korean alphabet (han'gŭl)
1592, 1598	Hideyoshi invasions
1627, 1636	Manchu invasions
1875–1876	Japan forced Korean ports to open to outside trade
1882	Trade treaty with United States
1883	First newspaper published
1895	Postal system established
1895	Sino-Japanese War (ended Korean suzerainty to China)
1899	First train; first telephone
1900	Electricity in Seoul
1904–1905	Russo-Japanese War (opened Korea to Japanese seizure)
1905	"Protective" treaty with Japan
1910–1945	Korea annexed into Japanese Colonial Empire
1919	March First Independence Movement
1945	Liberation from Japan and partition into North and South Korea
1950–1953	Korean War
1948–1960	Syngman Rhee, first president of South Korea
1963–1979	Park Chung Hee, president
1980–1987	Chun Doo Hwan, president
1988–1992	Roh Tae Woo, president
1993–1997	Kim Young Sam, president
1998–	Kim Dae Jung, president

‖ These are still extant and housed at Haeinsa Temple.

Appendix B

Traditional Symbols

The South Korean Flag

The South Korean flag incorporates an ancient Taoist design.

The unique symbolism that emblazons the Korean national flag is so striking that it is often selected when a program with a global theme must limit its choice of representative international flags to a handful. The original of the design was inherited from China and is so ancient it defies precise dating, yet it was not applied to the Korean flag until 1882. We recognize the yin-yang symbol (which Koreans call *ŭm-yang* or, collectively, *tae-gŭk*) in the center; placed at an angle in the corners around it are four of the sixty-four hexagrams referred to in chapter 3. The one with three solid bars in the upper left stands for heaven (also south), the three broken lines in the lower right for earth (also north), the one in the lower left represents fire (also east), and the one in the upper right, water (also west). As two opposite sets of the thirty-two hexagram pairs, they carry the implied message that harmony and balance represent the natural order of the universe.

During the thirty-five years that Japan ruled Korea, when the Korean flag was outlawed, many Koreans secretly kept flags hidden inside the plastered walls of their homes and were able to break them out and display them immediately upon liberation at the end of World War II.

The Chinese Zodiac*

The Chinese zodiac has also been adopted by Korea. It is based on the lunar calendar and is divided into twelve parts, each represented by an animal that is known for specific traits.

The twelve animals and their characteristic traits are listed below in the order they always follow:

Rat[†]	clever and crafty
Ox	serious and dutiful
Tiger	captivating and unpredictable
Rabbit[‡]	diplomatic and astute
Dragon	powerful and egocentric
Snake	beautiful and discerning
Horse	intelligent and capricious

---

[*] Consult a good reference book, like Theodora Lau's *The Handbook of Chinese Horoscopes* (New York: Harper and Row, 1979), for more complete information and for astrological readings. The traits assigned to the twelve animals on the list are taken from Ms. Lau's book.

[†] Asians do not attribute the derogatory or clownish characteristics we do to such animals as rats, snakes, and monkeys.

[‡] In Vietnam, the Cat is substituted for the Rabbit as the fourth animal, so in some English language books the rabbit is referred to as a cat (which it never is in Korea or China).

Sheep	gentle and wistful
Monkey	wily and deviously enchanting
Rooster	colorful and eccentric
Dog	loyal and realistic
Boar	sincere and generous

Thorough and complete astrological readings are much more complex than the brief listing of attributes given here, but if you want to know your own zodiac animal or whether it is currently the Year of the Horse or the Dragon or whatever, you may follow these simple directions to find out: the Rat is identified with the year 1960 and all years earlier or later in multiples of twelve. Therefore, if you were born in 1960, 1948, 1936, 1924, 1912 or 1972, 1984, 1996, 2008, etc., then your animal is the Rat. The Ox corresponds to the year 1961, and so forth, through all twelve animals in the order they are listed above.

Most Asians take their horoscopes seriously ("Why take a chance?"), and few would make an important decision—concerning the selection of a marriage partner, for example—without at least checking to see how their prospective mate's horoscope relates to their own. Many would also set their wedding date according to the astrologically most propitious time.

Other Important Korean Symbols

Like the symbolism on the flag and zodiac, Korea has borrowed many other symbols from China.

Longevity. Paramount among such symbols are several representing the Taoist-influenced concept of longevity, giving us some idea of how important the notion of longevity, which assumes being worthy of respect, is held to be. The pine tree, crane, deer, tortoise, and the Taoist mushroom and peach all symbolize immortality. You will see these visual representations of longevity everywhere.

Dragon. Another symbol we have come to associate with Asia, though Westerners usually misinterpret it as dangerous and destructive, is the dragon. In Asian countries, the dragon is a benevolent symbol, associated with water in all its forms— the ocean it inhabits, the rain it controls and with which it blesses our crops, and the mist, fog, and clouds that shield us from the heat of the sun. Its identification with rain has caused it to be associated with fertility and plenitude as well as with rejuvenation.

Phoenix. Often associated with the dragon is the imaginary bird known as the phoenix, which is usually illustrated as a combination of a pheasant (head and body) and peacock (tail feathers). It is said to make an appearance only in times of peace and prosperity, so when it is seen, it is thought to be a favorable omen and a validation of good times. The Chinese version of the phoenix, unlike the phoenix of Egyptian and ancient classical mythology in the West, does not rise from its own ashes.

The dragon became the symbol of the emperor of China and the phoenix, of the empress. Eventually the kings and queens of Korea also appropriated them as their signs of office, though, technically, they did not qualify to use them, since for at least six centuries they served under the suzerainty of the Chinese emperor. The imperial dragon was depicted with five claws, so you will often see several three- and four-toed dragons allocated to people of lesser rank. In today's Korea, the phoenix has been taken as the symbol of the presidency.

Tiger. Among all these Chinese-derived animals, it is interesting to discover one that is uniquely Korean in its interpretation—the tiger. Until as recently as two or three decades ago, the Siberian tiger was still occasionally found in Korea, and as of this writing, it is possible that a few still exist in the remote mountains of North Korea.

The tiger is the most beloved animal of Korean folk art. Although the tiger paintings almost always include magpies

in the scene, specialists in Korean folk art are not in agreement as to why. Some suspect that the mighty tiger really
represents the Korean yangban (bureaucrat) who held all the
power but who was often outwitted by the magpie, which
represents the lowly commoner who, like the magpie, managed through cleverness to remain out of reach of the tiger.
The magpie taunts the tiger much as the bluejay taunts house
cats. At any rate, both creatures are admired by Koreans.

Bat; the number 4. Two other symbols, also following the Chinese custom, are the bat and the number four.
Both of these are homophones (words
having the same sound as another
word but with a different meaning). In
both the Chinese and Korean languages, the word *bat* has exactly the
same sound as the Chinese character

for good fortune (*bok* in Korean), so
the bat is not for Koreans a frighten-
ing creature, as it is for some Americans. The other word is *four* (*sa*), because it is a homophone for *death*. This
means that it is avoided as unlucky.

These two stylized bats
are drawer pulls made of
brass and taken from a
Korean wooden chest of
the Chosŏn (Yi) Dy-
nasty.

Very much as many Westerners avoid the number thirteen,
so many Korean buildings are without a fourth floor or a room
number four. In Korea, one would be unlikely to give a gift of
four of anything. If you are observant, you will notice how
often Koreans give five of something when giving a small
number of things to another person (not a half-dozen, as
Americans would). Giving a Korean hostess four white flowers would, in fact, signify a double wish for death, since the
color white also signifies death in Korea.

Characters as Talismans. A few especially propitious Taoist-influenced Chinese characters are used frequently as talismans to convey their favorable meanings and as decorative
symbols. These include the character *su,* for longevity, and

bok, which we have already seen means good fortune (sometimes translated as blessings, bliss, or happiness). Below are shown several styles for signifying longevity, first in carefully written form, then in a freer, more cursive form, and finally in a more decorative derivation. These are followed by several similar examples of good fortune. Together, these two characters are referred to as *su-bok* (though never as *bok-su*), and they decorate everything from spoons to pillows.

The Chinese symbol for "double happiness" is also used by the Koreans to bring good luck to the owner of the objects it decorates. It is almost as popular as the characters for su and bok.

Several variations on the Chinese character for *su*, meaning "longevity." The last two examples have been so abstracted as to be unreadable, but Koreans recognize them as *su*, as you will also from now on.

Several variations on the Chinese character for *bok*, meaning good fortune. The last example is written in free cursive style.

"*The Four Gentlemen of Oriental Paint-ing.*" The final category of Korean sym-bols, also inherited from China, are what both the Chinese and Koreans call "the Four Gentlemen of Oriental Painting." They are not gentlemen at all; they are four plants: the plum blossom, wild or-chid, bamboo, and chrysanthemum. Each represents one of the four seasons, and each is rich in noble virtues.

This is the "double happiness" character.

The *plum blossom* represents winter, and its virtue is that it is the first blooming flower of the year, blooming in central China as early as the middle of January. Its symbolic message is that we should be like the plum blossom and have the deter-mination and courage to come to flower before any others.

The *wild orchid*, symbol of spring and one of the most beautiful of flowers, lives in the depths of the forest, drawing its sustenance from dead vegetation. It may live out its entire life without ever being seen by human eyes. Be like the orchid and bloom in all your beauty—even if no one ever notices your loveliness.

The *bamboo*, representing summer, is thought of as one of the tallest trees, and yet it is not a tree but a giant grass. It is so flexible that it can be blown flat to the ground, yet it does not break. Be like the bamboo, weather the storms and snap back up again without giving any evidence of the troubles you have experienced.

The last blooming flower of late autumn is the *chrysanthe-mum*. It is so hardy it can weather light frosts unscathed. Because of this, it is associated with the beauty and dignity of old age.

Lotus. Not part of this grouping, but another plant that represents an important symbol in Asia, is the lotus flower.

Its roots lie in the mud at the bottom of a lake, and it sends its stem up through the water to allow its beautiful flower to bloom in all its purity on the water's surface, in full view of the sun. Because of its ability to transform the ugliness of its origins into unsurpassed beauty, it is often associated with Buddhism or, more specifically, with working off an unfavorable karma and ultimately achieving enlightenment.

Appendix C

Traditional Social Customs

Korean Names and Name Seals

The Korean custom in name usage is to place the surname first, followed by the two-part given name. Many Koreans who are familiar with the Western tradition of placing the family name last, however, may follow the Western way when associating with foreigners—which can be confusing because there is no consistency of usage.

Women keep their maiden names after marriage. If the married woman has become at least partially familiar with Western customs, you may refer to her as Mrs. Kim, for example, using her husband's surname, but it is not something Koreans would do. As soon as the Korean wife has produced a male heir, people will refer to her as "So-and-So's mother."

In Korea, one's signature is not considered sure evidence that the person whose name appears on a document is necessarily the person who actually signed it. Koreans say, "Anyone could have signed that person's name, but only that person could have possession of his or her own seal." (Americans, of course, would reply, "Anyone could easily have the seal carved within an hour, but signatures are very hard to forge.") At any rate, if you are going to sign legal documents in Korea, you will need to have a seal stamp (*dojang*) cut for you. This will usually entail first having your name converted into a Korean name and that name assigned the proper Chinese characters (rather than being written in the phonetic *han'gŭl* script). Take great care to ask the most educated, literate Korean you can find to entrust with this task, for you will want to be given the most propitious name possible; yet, you will probably also want it to sound reasonably like your surname in English. Because of the differences between the two sound systems, however, you are only likely to achieve an approximation. If I may use my own surname—Kohls (written in Korean with Chinese characters)—as an example: when pronounced in English, my name has only one smooth syllable. But when transliterated into Korean, it becomes Koh-ŭl-soo. You will note that it conveniently now has three characters, as most Korean names do.

The Traditional Korean Home

From this point onward in Appendix C, much of what we will cover may be more descriptive of *traditional* Korean culture than of the Korean culture you will discover in the new millennium, and especially of the Korea you will observe in Seoul. Korea is rapidly abandoning its traditional culture for a modern Western version. Even so, it helps the newcomer to understand what it looked like before its transformation.

While in Korea you will be lucky if you are invited inside a traditional Korean home. As more and more city-based Koreans are living in apartments that are very much like American-style apartments, it becomes increasingly difficult to find a traditional-style Korean home. The Korean Folk Village in Suwŏn is rapidly becoming the only place where one can see such homes. Traditional homes were usually built in an "L" or a "U" shape, enclosing an inner courtyard.

One of the most interesting features of a traditional Korean home is the *ondol* floor, which gave Koreans radiant heating as early as the seventh century A.D., several centuries before its invention in the West. With the firebox built at one end of the room and the chimney at the opposite end, the warm smoke was channeled through under the floor, giving off its heat before it escaped. Koreans traditionally sat and slept on the floor, which was the warmest place on cold winter days. Sadly, fewer and fewer homes now have ondol floors in modern Korean apartment living.

Koreans remove their shoes before going inside their homes. Slippers are often provided, but they should be worn only in the parts of the home with bare wooden floors. Special slippers are also at the door into the bathroom for use only in the bathroom. (One of the easiest mistakes for Westerners to make is to absentmindedly wear the bathroom slippers into the living areas.)

By far the most enjoyable and least stressful relationship for an American to adjust to is to become a guest in a Korean household. You will, quite literally, be treated like royalty; your every whim will be catered to, even before you realize you are going to have that whim. Later, when the tables are turned and it is your turn to play the role of host to entertain your Korean guest, you will want to remember how to do so in the proper Korean way.

Food and Eating

Like *kimchi* (the hot and spicy pickled cabbage), much of Korean food is generously seasoned with garlic and red peppers, but many dishes are mild and bland, offering an excellent antidote if you happen to take too large a mouthful of kimchi or one of the other hot foods. (A mouthful of rice, by the way, works better than a drink of cold water to cool off a pepper-heated mouth.)

Since the various foods are to be eaten with chopsticks, they have been precut into bite-sized pieces. You will eventually become so skillful in handling chopsticks that you will swear they are the only instruments with which to pick up a single grain of rice or a lone peanut. The bowls of food are normally left sitting in the center of the table (rather than being passed around, as we do) and each person reaches across the table to pick up food, piece by piece, with his or her chopsticks.

Guests are not supposed to enter the kitchen in a Korean home. Of course, if the hostess, on her own initiative, invites you, feel free to go. But traditionally, Koreans were ashamed to compare their modest, originally dirt-floored kitchens with the gleaming kitchens pictured in American magazines. If you are really curious, and if you have developed a close friendship with a Korean housewife, you could ask her to please teach you how to prepare Korean food. In this way you could probably earn your way into her kitchen, especially if you offered to teach her how to make an American dish in exchange for her showing you how to prepare a Korean dish.

Other Korean formal mealtime rituals are equally important to follow. For one, Koreans typically dine with very little conversation, though they will sometimes carry on table talk for the benefit of their Western guests (all the time encouraging you to eat more). If the conversation lapses, don't feel obligated to get it going again. Other sounds, unexpected and often offensive to the Western ear, will be heard, however, especially slurping of soup and belching, both implied compliments signaling that you are enjoying or have enjoyed your meal. Don't, however, blow your nose at the dinner table. Koreans consider it disgusting and the height of rudeness. Another ritual is to always leave a little food on your plate to show that you have been provided with more than enough to eat. To clean the last grain of rice from your bowl will be taken as a sign that you want more. Watch also for the pleasant ritual of companions at the table filling each other's drinking glasses but never filling their own.

After the meal is finished, usually everyone will be asked to sing or perform in some way—perhaps with a simple magic trick or some other "performance" if you simply cannot bear to display your vocal skills, or lack thereof. The looser you are about this and the more you participate, the quicker you will find yourself able to break through the barriers of formality and be able to enter more fully into ingroup relationships.

There is a special drinking ritual that the American in Korea should be aware of. One person hands his liquor cup to another person, who receives the cup and holds it while the first person fills it with liquor. Then the second person drinks the contents and hands the cup back to the first person. They then reverse roles. This is obviously a way both of encouraging the other people to drink more and of building trust and enhancing friendships by drinking from the same cup.

Toothpicks may be used at the table (violating a rule of etiquette in the United States), but you must shield your mouth with your left hand as you complete this hygienic operation with your right.

All of the above will be useful if you are invited to a Korean home. Truth is, however, that traditionally, Koreans did not entertain socially in their homes. Instead, they invited their guests to a well-chosen restaurant or to a teahouse or coffeeshop. Koreans who invite you home for a meal are breaking with Korean tradition because they have become familiar with American customs and perhaps because they also know that Americans are curious to see the inside of a Korean home.

Foreign businessmen are often entertained at an all-male kisaeng (pronounced "key-seng") party, where the Korean counterparts of geishas pour their drinks, see that they have plenty to eat, and entertain them with singing and dancing.

Holidays

Eleven official holidays (which are marked with an asterisk in the list that follows) are recognized by the government of South Korea. Some of the holidays are tied to the lunar calendar, so those will vary from year to year on the solar-based Gregorian calendar, which both Korea and the United States now use.

New Year's Day*	January 1–3
Lunar New Year (Folklore Day)*	End of January to early March, same date as Chinese New Year's Day
Independence Movement Day* (Commemorating the independence movement of March 1, 1919)	March 1
Labor Day*	March 10
Hanshik Day (lunar) (A day to visit ancestral graves with offerings of food and wine)	Early April
Arbor Day	April 5
Buddha's Birthday (lunar)*	April or May
Children's Day	May 5
Memorial Day*	June 6
Farmer's Day	June 15
Tano Day (lunar) (A day to offer prayers for good harvest and to visit ancestral graves)	Late June
Constitution Day* (Celebrates the adoption of the constitution in 1948)	July 17
Liberation Day* (Liberation from Japan at end of World War II)	August 15
Chusŏk (lunar)* (Korean Thanksgiving Day or Harvest Moon Festival)	Late September/early October
Armed Forces Day	October 1
National Foundation Day* (Marks founding of Korea by mythical Tan'gun, 2333 B.C.)	October 3
Han'gŭl Day (Celebrates adoption of phonetic alphabet in 1446)	October 9
Christmas Day*	December 25

Birthday, Marriage, and Funeral Customs

Nowadays, many modern Koreans follow American traditions in celebrating their birthdays by giving gifts, having a
birthday cake, and so forth, but traditionally, Koreans observed only three birth-related celebrations. The first is the
day commemorating the completion of the first one hundred
days of life; the second is the first full year after birth; and the
final one is not until the sixtieth birthday, called the *hwangap*
celebration (see page 105 for further discussion) to recognize
that the person has completed the "normal" sixty-year cycle
(five times through the twelve-year zodiac).

At the one-year birthday celebration, the young boy (there
is no comparable one-year birthday celebration for girls) is
seated in front of a table containing several objects to see
which one he will pick up first. If he takes the writing brush,
he will grow up to become a scholar; if he chooses the money,
a businessman; if the knife, a soldier; if the food, a government official; if the thread, he will live a long life. Although
this is done in fun, considerable significance is often attached
to the prediction.

Marriage was, and to a large extent remains, a societal
institution in which everyone is expected to take part. Only
the mentally disabled or severely physically handicapped are
excused. A male was not considered an adult, regardless of his
age, until he married.

In the "old days" one saw no public display of affection
between men and women. One did not even see a young man
and woman walking together before marriage and rarely after,
and on those rare occasions the wife was expected to follow
her husband two or three steps behind and slightly to his left.
Unmarried sons and daughters were expected to live at home
until they wed, and it was the duty of the parents to arrange
their children's marriages. The Western custom of dating
has, of course, arrived in modern Korea, but one is still more
likely to see young people in *sandwich dates*; that is, two or

three members of each sex going out together as a group, rather than one male pairing off with one female.

The strictly arranged marriage (*chungmae*), where the two young people were not introduced to each other or even allowed to see one another until their wedding day, is almost nonexistent today. What has developed in its place is most often a compromise arrangement, where the young people are first selected for each other, usually by a professional match-maker (and usually including the checking of horoscopes to see that they are compatible), and then they are introduced and allowed to date a few times (or at least to meet once) to see if they want to go through with the wedding. Nevertheless, marriage is still considered to be a binding together not of two individuals but of two families.

More and more love marriages (*yŏnmae*) are taking place these days and in urban areas are usually held in huge wedding halls in full Western style, complete with bridal gowns and all the trimmings, including professional photographers and even masters of ceremony at the reception.

In addition to taking a wife, which was his overriding duty, the traditional Korean man had options not readily accepted by every culture. He was free to take as many other wives or concubines as he could afford. There were also kisaeng entertainers and prostitutes available for his pleasure, with society's blessing. A number of influences in Korean society have changed this situation considerably. Christianity has brought new concepts of morality, as has increasing familiarity with Western feminism. An awareness of AIDS has also had its part in reshaping the sexual practices of Korean males.

The Korean wife is not considered to have fulfilled her obligation until she has given birth to a male heir, and the couple that has produced only female offspring will be pitied for not having a son to carry on the husband's lineage, to provide for them in their old age, and to show the proper respect for them after their deaths by performing the required ancestral rites.

The preference for a male heir, by and large, remains to this day.* In historic times, failure to produce a male was grounds for divorce. Most Koreans will go to any length to ensure the birth of a son, including prayers offered in Buddhist temples or ancient Korean animistic rites, prayers spoken before sacred rock formations or written out and tied to the branches of trees that are considered to have special magical powers.

As noted earlier, the unmarried foreign man or woman in Korea will be hounded with persistent questions as to why he or she is not yet married. The unmarried woman, in particular, will be constantly worried over. She will likely even be asked why her father has allowed her to leave his home and country without being married.

The childless foreign couple working in Korea will be asked over and over again why they have no children. The answer "We have decided not to have any children" is absolutely impossible for Koreans to understand. Some wives have found, provided they are still young enough, that the only answer that is somewhat within the Korean realm of understanding is "We have decided to wait until we return home to have our first child so that we will be near our parents." If this is a cop-out, so be it. After enough harassment, you may find yourself willing enough to silence the harassers by using this excuse.

In Korea the "Death Day," the date a person dies, is traditionally remembered and honored more than that person's birthday. Though white was the traditional color for mourning, modern urban mourners have adopted the Western practice of wearing black. People are obligated to visit the graves of ancestors and to perform the annual rituals, especially at New Year's and on the harvest festival of Chusŏk. Largely

---

* The ready availability of the ultrasonogram has been the cause of an increase in abortions of female fetuses, resulting in an imbalance in the ratio of male to female babies born.

gone now are the colorful funeral processions that could still be seen in rural areas thirty or forty years ago, with the banners that preceded the hand-carried bier fluttering in the wind and announcing the name and rank of the deceased. The bier itself was covered with a brightly colored cloth canopy and paper flowers. Finally, bringing up the rear, came the loudly wailing male descendants dressed in hemp sackcloth. What has remained, and will likely do so for some time to come, is the seriousness with which the eldest son assumes his new responsibilities as head of the household and the faithfulness with which the person's close relatives perform their gravesite rituals.

It is widely believed by Koreans that to fail to choose the proper place for a loved one's grave will cause the living heirs to have bad luck. One of the remedies to end such bad luck is to employ a professional geomancer to choose a new, luckier spot and to rebury one's ancestor there. As you travel throughout the countryside you will see hundreds of the small rounded mounds that mark individual graves.

Space and Time Concepts

The American visitor to Korea will be struck immediately by the density of its population and the degree to which Koreans live in compact spaces. A small rural town that Americans might on first glance judge to have a population of around five hundred will have five thousand residents. This is partially because there are sixteen times as many people per square mile in Korea as in the United States and partially because most collectivist societies do not feel a need for as much personal space as Americans do. Homes do not normally have separate, private rooms for each family member, and the same room becomes the living room, dining room, or bedroom, depending on what carry-in furnishings it contains at the moment. The typical office worker in the U.S. usually prefers a private office; in Korea the open "bull-pen" arrangement is much more common, seemingly preferred for the togetherness it engenders.

Interestingly, the personal space Koreans need—in other words, the culturally determined bubble of space around them beyond which penetration becomes intrusion—is not much different from the American bubble. It is slightly smaller, but not so small as that of Latin Americans and Arabs, who, to North Americans, always seem to stand too close. Koreans are, however, readier to brush or bump past each other in public without excusing themselves than Americans are. You are likely to notice, for instance, as you walk down a busy street in Seoul or Pusan, that Koreans bump into you a lot more than people do in the average American city.

You will also encounter people running on "Korean time" for whom the keeping of appointments is more casual than in the United States. This holds much less true for modern-day Korean business executives, who, if anything, are even more time- or at least appointment-conscious than the stereotypical American. Best advice: be on time for all business meetings in Korea, but don't be surprised if occasionally a Korean is late. On the other hand, few Koreans share the Americans' excessive worry over time and how it is used or the degree to which it is wasted.

Westerners, generally, schedule one event or appointment at a time and may partition their days into half-hour, or even fifteen-minute, segments. Koreans are able to cope with numerous actions occurring simultaneously and overlapping.

Appendix D

Aspects of Korean Culture Worth Exploring

One of my hidden agendas in writing this book has been to pique your interest in all things Korean. The major portion of this book has been focused on explaining, in ways that would best communicate to most Westerners, the logic behind the radically different values, assumptions, and thought processes of the Korean worldview. Here in Appendix D I deal not with those fundamentals of Korean culture but with "all things Korean." In many ways, these represent the fun parts about discovering what makes Korea and Koreans tick.

Although my agenda may have been hidden until now, my way of achieving it is quite straightforward. Experience has shown there are two external clues to knowing which particular foreigners are likely to excel in their adjustment to Korea: (1) those who make the strongest attempt to speak as much Korean as they can (not necessarily those who do the best in completely mastering this difficult language, but those who put forth the greatest effort) and (2) those who are demonstrably the most curious in their exploration of every aspect of the Korean culture. It is toward the achievement of this second goal that Appendices B, C, and D have been included.

229

Here is a partial list of topics to ask Koreans about. Some of them might spark a special interest or perhaps a visit to a museum (to inspect Korean celadon ceramics, for example) or a trip to see the Korean Folk Village in Suwŏn together with a Korean friend. The items presented below are listed in random order, and you are encouraged to simply scan the list and explore them in the order of your preference.

- Radiant-heated (ondol) floors
- *Sijo* (pronounced "Shee-jo") poetry
- Calligraphy
- Classical Chinese-style painting
- Korean temples, palaces, gardens, pavilions, gates, and tombs
- Traditional costumes (*hanbok*)
- National holidays (and the traditions accompanying them)
- Korean dance
- Masked drama and puppet performances
- Flag symbolism
- National anthem
- Korean food and cooking
- Fortune-telling, astrology, and geomancy
- Shaman (*Mudang*) ceremonies (*kut*)
- Visual arts of the various periods (at Korean museums)
- Games (e.g., *yut*, *paduk*, kite flying, high swings, and seesaw jumping boards)
- March 1, 1919 independence movement
- Traditional wedding, birth, and funeral customs
- Korean language
- Chinese herbal medicine

- Ginseng
- Acupuncture and moxibustion
- Court music (in the T'ang Dynasty Chinese tradition)
- *Pansori* ballads
- Mulberry paper and papermaking
- Name seals (*dojang*)
- *Ddŏk* stamps
- Korean creation myth and Tan'gun
- Korean folk painting
- Korean proverbs
- Korean archery
- Native religions
- Early Korean achievements in printing/movable metal type (200 years before Gutenberg)
- Kisaeng (geisha) tradition
- *Taekwŏndo*
- Korean wrestling
- Village markets (on five-day schedule)
- Roof tiles
- Rubbings of bas-relief sculpture (*takbŏn*)
- Lacquerware (with mother-of-pearl inlay)
- Brassware (including "bell brass")
- *Wangŭl* mats
- Folding fans
- Traditional musical instruments (especially the *kayagŭm*)
- Acrobatic troupes
- Korean family registers/family trees (*Jokbo*)

- King Sejong's phonetic alphabet (han'gŭl)
- Chinese characters
- Traditional Korean furniture, especially Korean chests
- Celadon ceramics of the Koryŏ Dynasty
- Asia's oldest existing astronomical observatory (Chŏmsŏngdae) in Kyŏngju
- Large cast bronze bells (of Unified Shilla Period)
- Admiral Yi Sun Shin's tortoise ships
- Buddhism
- Confucianism
- Taoism
- Rami and hemp cloth
- Sixty-year life cycle
- Ancestor veneration
- Korean embroidery
- Making kimchi
- Asian zodiac
- Ornamental knots
- Chejudo Island
- Kyŏngju (ancient capital of Shilla Dynasty)
- *Pojagi* (wrapping cloths)

Appendix E

Aspects of American Culture Worth Explaining to Koreans

The other half of culture sharing is for you to provide information about the United States to your Korean cultural informant (the Korean national who explains to you the multiple aspects of Korean culture that are suggested in Appendix D) and other Koreans who may ask you about the U.S.

I know from past experience that many American MBAs, who know everything they need to know to manage a complex business organization, feel they know far too little about U.S. history or American culture to explain either to foreigners (who in many cases may already know more about these subjects than many Americans do). If that is the case, you might want to call on some of your fellow expatriates to help you fill in the gaps in your knowledge. A quick brainstorming session with them before you all meet together to inform your Korean counterpart or colleagues about life in the United States will demonstrate this may well be a job where two (or three) heads are, indeed, better than one. An informal discussion among yourselves, with each of you contributing examples from your own lives, then an informal discussion with the Korean culture informant, then answering any questions he or she might have will be more informative than you can imagine. With two or three Americans providing examples from their personal experience, you will be able to offer the best evidence of a very American belief: that there is not one single American reality but multiple realities that are as different as our individual personalities are different from each other.

Start with topics that you are confident you know well—perhaps explaining how American football differs from soccer, for example—and with a few successes under your belt, you will find it easier to move on to other, more complex topics. And don't hesitate to call on members of the entire American expat community to help you out.

- Basic American values (such as those in the right-hand column of the Kohls Values Continuum in chapter 4)
- Overview of American history
- Physical environment
- Regional differences
- Political system
- Family life/New Age family structures
- Male-female relationships
- Dating/marriage/divorce
- Young people/old people
- Classes in a "classless society"
- Open as compared with closed societies
- From conservative to liberal/from Hippie to Yuppie to New Age to Generation X and beyond
- Minority cultures: African Americans, Hispanic Americans (Latinos), Asian Americans, and Native Americans (American Indians), among others

- Problems faced by modern U.S. society
- Urban life/suburban life
- Labor
- Agriculture/rural life
- Economy and financial institutions
- Commerce and business
- Working for an American company
- Educational system
- Studying at an American university
- Religion in America
- Welfare system
- Justice and legal services
- Health care and medical services
- Science and technology
- Media and communications systems
- The arts (painting, sculpture, architecture, vocal music, instrumental music, dance, drama, poetry)
- Literature*
- Sports
- American holidays

---

* Literature has been distinguished from the other arts because (like American history) it is often considered a separate subject by Korean English majors, and the volume of literary texts and American authors is so huge.

Bibliography

Encyclopaedic Handbooks

Cho, Byung K. *Korean Culture, Tourism and Language: For Everything You Need to Know about Korea*. Green Bay: Cho's Black Belt Academy, 1992.

Handbook of Korea. Korean Overseas Information Service, Ministry of Culture and Information, Republic of Korea. Seoul: Samsung Moonwha Press, latest edition.

Korea Annual: A Comprehensive Handbook on Korea. Seoul: Yonhap News Agency, latest edition.

Korea: Its Land, People and Culture of All Ages. Seoul: Hakwonsa, 1960.

Koreana: Korean Culture and Heritage. 4 vols. Seoul: The Korea Foundation, 1994–1998.

Pratt, Keith, and Richard Rutt. *Korea: A Historical and Cultural Dictionary*. Durham, England: Curzon Press, 1999.

Korea, General

Allen, Horace. *Things Korean*. Seoul: Royal Asiatic Society Korea Branch, 1980.

An, Tai Sung. *North Korea: A Political Handbook*. Wilmington, DE: Scholarly Resources, 1983.

Buzzo, Adrian. *the Guerilla Dynasty: Politics and Leadership in North Korea*. Boulder, CO: Westview Press, 1999.

Castley, Robert. *Korea's Economic Miracle: The Crucial Role of Japan*. New York: St. Martin's Press, 1997.

Covell, Jon Carter. *Korea's Cultural Roots*. Elizabeth, NJ: Hollym International Corporation, 1985.

Covell, Jon Carter, and Alan Covell. *Korean Impact on Japanese Culture: Japan's Hidden History*. Elizabeth, NJ: Hollym International Corporation, 1984.

Crane, Paul. *Korean Patterns*. Seoul, Royal Asiatic Society Korea Branch, 1986.

Davis, Lucile. *South Korea*. Countries of the World Series. Mankato, MN: Bridgestone Books, 1999.

Eberstadt, Nicholas. *The End of North Korea*. Washington, DC: American Enterprise Institute, 1999.

Edwards, Paul M. *The Korean War*. Malabar, FL: Krieger Publishing, 1999.

Gibney, Frank B. *Korea's Quiet Revolution: From Garrison State to Democracy*. New York: Walker and Company, 1993.

Grant, Bruce. *Korean Proverbs*. Seoul: Wu Ah Dong, 1985.

Ha, Tae Hung. *Maxims and Proverbs of Old Korea*. Seoul: Yonsei University Press, 1964.

Hoare, James, and Susan Pares. *Korea: An Introduction*. New York: Kegan Paul International, 1988.

Hunter, Helen-Louise, and Stephen J. Solarz. *Kim Il-Song's North Korea*. Westport, CT: Praeger, 1999.

Images of Korea (videocassette). Seoul: Korea Foundation, 1993.

Kim, Chong-Won, Joungwon Alexander Kim, and Junwan A. Kim. *Divided Korea: The Politics of Development*. Cambridge, MA: Harvard University Press, 1999.

Kim, Eun Mee, ed. *The Four Asian Tigers: Economic Development and the Global Political Economy*. San Diego: Academic Press, 1998.

Kim, Il Pyong, ed. *Two Koreas in Transition: Implications for U.S. Policy*. St. Paul, MN: Paragon House, 1998.

Lee, Charles S. *North Korea: Country Background Report*. Washington, DC: Congressional Research Service, Library of Congress, 1990.

Lee, O. Young. *In This Earth and in That Wind*. Elizabeth, NJ: Hollym International Corporation, 1967.

Lee, O. Young, et al. *Things Korean*. Boston: Charles Tuttle, 1999.

Lee, Peter H., and William Theodore DeBary, eds. *Sources of Korean Tradition*. vols. 1 and 2. New York: Columbia University Press, 1996, 1997.

Lee, Yur-Bok, and Wayne Patterson, eds. *Korean-American Relations: 1866–1997*. Albany, NY: State University of New York Press, 1998.

Lim, Haeren. *Korea's Growth and Industrial Transformation*. New York: St. Martin's Press, 1998.

McCune, Shannon. *Korea's Heritage: A Regional and Social Geography*. Rutland, VT: Charles E. Tuttle, 1956.

Nash, Amy K. *North Korea*. Major World Nations Series. Broomall, PA: Chelsea House, 1997.

Oh, John Kie-Chiang. *Korean Politics: The Quest for Democratization and Economic Development*. Ithaca, NY: Cornell University Press, 1999.

Osgood, Cornelius. *The Koreans and Their Culture*. New York: Ronald Press, 1951 (anthropological study of traditional village life in Korea).

Park, Myung Seok. *Communication Styles in Two Different Cultures: Korean and American*. Seoul: Han Shin Publishing Co., 1979.

Ricci, Richard B., ed. *Living in Korea*. Seoul: American Chamber of Commerce in Korea, 1981.

Savada, Andrea M. *North Korea: A Country Study*. 4th ed. Washington, DC: Library of Congress, 1994.

Scalapino, Robert A., ed. *North Korea Today*. New York: Praeger, 1963.

Solberg, S. E. *The Land and People of Korea*. New York: HarperCollins, 1991.

South Korea: A Country Study. 4th ed. Washington, DC: Library of Congress, 1992.

Suh, Dae Sook. *Kim Il Sung: The North Korean Leader*. New York: Columbia University Press, 1988.

Suh, Dae Sook, and Chae-Jin Lee, eds. *North Korea After Kim Il Sung*. Boulder, CO: Lynne Rienner Publishers, 1998.

Yang, Seung Mok. *Korean Customs and Etiquette*. Seoul: Moon Yang Gak, 1990.

Yang, Won Dal. *Korean Ways, Korean Mind*. Seoul: Tamgu Dang, 1982.

Yim, Yong Soon. *Politics of Korean Unification*. Seoul: Research Center for Peace and Unification of Korea, 1988.

History

Cumings, Bruce. *Korea's Place in the Sun: A Modern History*. New York: W. W. Norton, 1997.

Deuchler, Martina. *The Confucian Transformation of Korea*. A *Study of Society and Ideology*. Cambridge, MA: Harvard University, 1992.

Eckert, Carter, et al. *Korea, Old and New: A History*. Seoul: published for the Korea Institute, Harvard University, by Ilchokak, 1999.

Goulden, Joseph. *Korea: The Untold Story of the* [Korean] *War*. Honolulu: University of Hawaii Press, 1982.

Han, Woo Keun. *The History of Korea*. Honolulu: University of Hawaii Press, 1971.

Henthorn, William E. *A History of Korea*. New York: Free Press, 1971.

Korea, Old and New: A History. Seoul: Korea Institute, Harvard University, 1990.

Lee, Chang Soo. *Modernization of Korea and the Impact on the West*. Los Angeles: East Asia Studies Center, University of California Press, 1981.

Lee, Ki Baik. *A New History of Korea*. Cambridge, MA: Yenching Institute, Harvard University Press, 1984.

Lee, Peter H. *Sources of Korean Tradition*. vols 1 and 2. New York: Columbia University Press, 1996, 1997.

Macdonald, Donald S. *The Koreans: Contemporary Politics and Society*. Boulder, CO: Westview Press, 1996.

Nahm, Andrew C. *Korea: Tradition and Transformation: A History of the Korean People*. Elizabeth, NJ: Hollym International Corporation, 1988.

———. *A Panorama of 5,000 Years: Korean History*. Elizabeth, NJ: Hollym International Corporation, 1989.

Oberdorfer, Don. *The Two Koreas: A Contemporary History*. Reading, MA: Addison Wesley, 1997.

Oliver, Robert T. *A History of the Korean People in Modern Times: 1800 to Present*. Cranberry, NJ: University of Delaware Press, 1993.

Pak, Chong Hwa. *King Sejong: A Novel*. New York: Larchwood Publications, 1980.

Park, Yune Hee. *Admiral Yi Sun Shin and His Turtleboat Armada*. Seoul: Hanjin Publishing, 1978.

Rees, David. *A Short History of Modern Korea*. New York: Hippocrene Books, 1991.

Rutt, Richard. *History of the Korean People*. Seoul: Taewon Publishing Company, 1972 (revision of James Gale's earlier book on Korean history).

Wylie, Hugh, and Wongyang Koh. *Korea: A Timeless Beauty*. Toronto: Royal Ontario Museum, 1999.

Religion/Philosophy

Choi, Min Hong. *Comparative Philosophy: Western and Korean Philosophies Compared*. Seoul: Sung Moon Sa, 1980.

Clark, Charles Allen. *Religions of Old Korea*. Seoul: Christian Literature Society, 1961.

Clark, Donald N. *Christianity in Modern Korea*. Lanham, MD: University Press of America, 1986.

Grayson, James. *Korea: A Religious History*. Oxford: Oxford University Press, 1989.

Hong, Jun Shik. *International Cultural Foundation: Buddhist Culture in Korea*. Seoul: Sisa Yongo Sa, 1982.

Huhm, Halla Pai. *Kut: Korean Shamanist Rituals*. Elizabeth, NJ: Hollym International Corporation, 1985.

Kim, Duk Hwang. *A History of Religion in Korea*. Seoul: Daeji Moonhwa Sa, 1988.

Palmer, Spencer J. *Confucian Rituals in Korea*. Seoul: Rochin Jai, 1984.

Takeuchi, Yoshinori, ed. *Buddhist Spirituality: Later China, Korea, Japan, and the Modern World* (World Spirituality, vol. 9). New York: Crossroad Publishing, 1999.

Business/Economics

American Chamber of Commerce in Korea. *Business Climate in Korea*. Seoul: American Chamber of Commerce, latest edition.

Cho, Soon. *The Dynamics of Korean Economic Development*. Washington, DC: Institute for International Economics, 1994.

Chung, Kae H., and Hak Chong Lee, eds. *Korean Managerial Dynamics*. New York: Praeger, 1989.

De Mente, Boye. *Korean Etiquette and Ethics in Business*. Chicago: NTC Business Books, 1989.

Ernst and Young. *Doing Business in Korea*. New York: Ernst and Young International, latest edition.

Hawley, Samuel J. *Help Wanted—Korea: The Insider's Guide to Working and Living in Prosperous, Exotic South Korea*. Greenport, NY: Pilot Books, 1997.

Hinkleman, Edward G., series ed. *Korea Business: The Portable Encyclopedia for Doing Business with Korea*. San Rafael, CA: World Trade Press, 1994 (contains much information not easily found elsewhere on foreign investment, import and export policies, business law, financial institutions, corporate taxation, personal taxation, etc.).

International Trade Administration. *How to Market in Korea*. Washington, DC: U.S. Department of Commerce (International Trade Administration), 1990 (available from U.S. Government Printing Office).

Jang, Song Hyon, ed. *The Key to Successful Business in Korea*. Seoul: Yong Ahn Publishing, 1988.

Kearney, Robert P. *The Warrior Worker: The History and Challenge of South Korea's Economic Miracle*. New York: Henry Holt, 1991.

Kim, Dong Ki, and Linsu Kim, eds. *Management Behind Industrialization: Readings in Korean Business*. Seoul: Korea University Press, 1989.

Kim, Eun Young. *A Cross-Cultural Reference of Business Practices in a New Korea*. Westport, CT: Greenwood Press, 1997.

Korea Business Directory. Seoul: Korea Chamber of Commerce and Industry, latest edition. (Information on 5,000 major Korean companies and 2,000 economic organizations).

Korea for the Business Traveler. Hauppauge, NY: Barron's, 1994.

Korea Trade Publications. *Trade with Korea*. Seoul: Korea Trade Promotion Corporation, 1991–1992 (available from Korea Trade Promotion Corporation, 460 Park Avenue, New York, NY 10022).

KOTRA. *How to do Business with Korea.* Seoul: KOTRA
(Korea Trade-Investment Promotion Agency), 1996.
Leppert, Paul. *Doing Business with the Koreans.* Fremont, CA:
Jain Publishing, 1990.
Price Waterhouse. *Doing Business in Korea.* Los Angeles: Price
Waterhouse World Firm Limited, latest edition.
Steers, Richard M., Yoo Keun Shin, and Gerald R. Ungion.
The Chaebol: Korea's New Industrial Might. New York:
Harper and Row, 1989.
Whitehill, Arthur, ed. *Doing Business in Korea.* New York:
Nichols Publishing, 1987.

Guidebooks, General

Adams, Edward B. *Korea Guide.* Seoul: International Publish-
ing House, 1976.
————. *Kyongju Guide: Cultural Spirit of Shilla in Korea.* Seoul:
International Tourist Publishing, 1983.
Hur, Sonja Vegdahl, and Ben Seunghwa Hur. *Culture Shock!
Korea.* Portland, OR: Graphic Arts Center, 1993.
Nilsen, Robert. *South Korea Handbook.* 2d ed. Emeryville,
CA: Avalon Publishing, 1997.

Art/Architecture

Adams, Edward B. *Palaces of Seoul.* Seoul International Tour-
ist Publishing, 1982.
————. *Art Treasures of Seoul.* Seoul: International Tourist
Publishing, 1982.
————. *Korea's Pottery Heritage.* Seoul: Seoul International
Publishing, 1987.
Asian Art Museum of San Francisco: 5,000 Years of Korean Art.
Seoul: Samhwa Printing Company, 1979.
Chung, Yang-Mo, et al. *Arts of Korea.* New York: Metropoli-
tan Museum, 1998.

Goepper, Roger, and Roderick Whitfield. *Treasures from Korea*. London: The British Museum, 1984.

Gompertz, Godfrey St. G. M. *Korean Celadon and Other Wares of the Koryo Period*. London: Faber and Faber, 1963.

Kim, Chewon. *Treasures of Korean Art*. New York: H. N. Abrams, 1966.

Kim, Chewon, and Lena Kim Lee. *Arts of Korea*. Tokyo: Kodansha International, 1974.

Kim, Won Yong. *Art and Archaeology of Ancient Korea*. Seoul: Taekwang Publishing, 1986.

Kim, Won Yong, Han Byong-Sam and Chin Hong-Sop. *The Arts of Korea*. 6 vols. Seoul: Dong Hwa Publishing, 1979.

Kim, Won Yong, et al. *Korean Art Treasures*. Seoul: Yekyong Publications, 1986 (authoritative sections on painting, sculpture, metalwork, earthenware, pottery and porcelain, architecture, and furniture, written by leading experts in each area).

McCune, Evelyn. *The Arts of Korea: An Illustrated History*. Rutland, VT: Charles E. Tuttle, 1962.

McKillop, Beth. *Korean Art and Design*. London: Victoria and Albert Museum, 1992.

National Gallery of Art, Washington, DC. *Masterpieces of Korean Art*. Boston: T. O. Metcalf, 1957.

National Museum of Korea: Selected Treasures of National Museums of Korea. Seoul: Samhwa Printing Company, 1988.

Portal, Jane. *Korea: Art and Archaeology*. London: Thames and Hudson, 2000.

A Short History of Korean Art. Seoul: Art Historical Association of Korea, 1970.

Yamato Bunkakan Museum: Korean Buddhist Paintings of the Koryo Dynasty. Nara, Japan: Yamato Bunkakan Press, 1978.

Folk Art

Moes, Robert. *Auspicious Spirits: Korean Folk Painting and Related Objects*. New York: International Exhibitions Foundation, 1983.

Onyang Folk Museum: The Folkcrafts of Korea. Seoul: Kyemongsa, 1980.

Zo, Za Dong. *Guardians of Happiness: Shamanistic Traditions in Korean Folk Painting*. Seoul: Royal Asiatic Society Korea Branch, 1982.

————. *Korean Tiger: An Exhibition of Korean Folk Painting*. Seoul: Emille Museum, 1984.

Music/Dance

Ha, Tae Hung. *Korea Sings: Folk and Popular Music and Lyrics*. Seoul: Yonsei University Press, 1960.

History of Korean Music. Seoul: Ministry of Culture and Information, Republic of Korea, no date.

Korean Dances (videocassette). Seoul: Korean Film Production, 1977.

Korean Musical Instruments. Seoul: National Classical Music Institute of Korea, 1982.

Lee, Hye Gu. *An Introduction to Korean Music and Dance*. Seoul: Royal Asiatic Society Korea Branch, 1977.

The Mask Dances of Korea (videocassette). Seoul: Korean Film Production, 1984.

Pansori: Korean Dramatic Songs (videocassette). Seoul: Korean Film Production, 1991.

In addition to the items mentioned above, there are several excellent recordings of Korean music available.

Literature/Poetry

Best Love Poems of Korea Selected for Foreigners. Elizabeth, NJ: Hollym International Corporation, 1984.

The Classical Poetry of Korea. Seoul: Korean Culture and Arts Foundation, 1981.

Ha, Tae Hung. *Folk Tales of Old Korea.* Seoul: Yonsei University Press, 1984.

———. *Poetry and Music of the Classic Age.* Seoul: Yonsei University Press, 1986.

Hong, Myoung Hee. *Korean Short Stories.* Seoul: Ilji Sa, 1975.

Hyon, Joon Shik. *Modern Korean Short Stories.* New York: Larchwood Publications, 1981.

Hyun, Peter. *Korea's Favorite Tales and Lyrics.* Seoul: Seoul International Publishing, 1986.

Kim, Chong-un, and Bruce Fulton. *A Ready-Made Life: Early Masters of Modern Korean Fiction.* Honolulu: University of Hawaii Press, 1998.

Kim, Gi Dong. *The Classical Novels of Korea.* Seoul: Korean Culture and Arts Foundation, 1981.

Kim, Jai Hium. *Classical Korean Poetry.* Seoul: Hanshin Publishing, 1987.

———. *Master Sijo Poems from Korea.* Seoul: Sisa Yongo Sa, 1982.

Kim, Jong Won. *Postwar Korean Short Stories: An Anthology.* Seoul: Seoul National University Press, 1974.

Lee, Peter H. *Anthology of Korean Literature from Early Times to the Nineteenth Century.* Honolulu: University of Hawaii Press, 1981.

———. *Korean Literature: Topics and Themes.* Tucson, AZ: University of Arizona Press, 1965.

McGreal, Ian Philip, ed. *Great Literature of the Eastern World.* New York: HarperCollins, 1996.

Pihl, Marshall. *Listening to Korea: A Korean Anthology.* New York: Praeger, 1973.

———. *Land of Exile: Contemporary Korean Fiction.* New York: M. E. Sharpe, 1993.

Riordan, James. *Korean Folk Tales.* New York: Oxford University Press Children's Books, 1994.

Rutt, Richard. *The Bamboo Grove: An Introduction to Sijo*. Berkeley: University of California Press, 1971.

———. *An Introduction to the Sijo: a Form of Short Korean Poem*. Seoul: Royal Asiatic Society Korea Branch, 1958.

Sim, Chai Hong. *Fragrance of Spring: The Story of Choon Hyang*. Seoul: Pochin Jai, 1970.

Zong, In Sob. *Folk Tales from Korea*. Elizabeth, NJ: Hollym International Corporation, 1986.

Furniture

Pai, Man Sil, and Edward Reynolds Wright. *Korean Furniture: Elegance and Tradition*. Tokyo: Kodansa, 1984.

Wickman, Michael. *Korean Chests*. Seoul: Seoul International Publishing, 1978.

Cuisine

Cho, Joong Ok. *Home Style Korean Cooking in Pictures*. Tokyo: Shufunotomo, 1981.

Choe, Ji Sook. *Korean Cooking for Everyone*. Tokyo: Joie, 1986.

Chu, Woul Young. *Traditional Korean Cuisine*. Seoul: Kyohak Sa, 1985.

Ha Sook Jeong. *Traditional Korean Cooking*. Seoul: Chong Woo Publishing, 1983.

Hyun, Judy. *The Korean Cookbook*. Elizabeth, NJ: Hollym International Corporation, 1986.

Marks, Copeland, and Manjo Kim. *The Korean Kitchen*. San Francisco: Chronicle Books, 1999.

Noh, Chin Hwa. *Healthful Korean Cooking*. Elizabeth, NJ: Hollym International Corporation, 1985 (meats and poultry).

———. *Low Fat Korean Cooking*. Elizabeth, NJ: Hollym International Corporation, 1985 (fish, shellfish, vegetables).

————. *Traditional Korean Cooking.* Elizabeth, NJ: Hollym International Corporation, 1985 (snacks and side dishes).

Rutt, Joan, and Sandra Mattielli, eds. *Lee Wade's Korean Cookery.* Elizabeth, NJ: Hollym International Corporation, 1985.

Many videocassettes, slides, and recordings are available on free loan from the Korea Cultural Center, 5505 Wilshire Boulevard, Los Angeles, CA 90036. Tel. 213-936-7144/Fax. 213-936-5712. www.kccla.org lists their video holdings in several categories, including:

- General information on Korea
- Cultural Treasures
- Korean Language
- Religion
- Traditional Customs
- Painting
- Music
- Dance
- Sports
- Tourism
- Industry and Manufacturing
- Feature Films

Other Useful Websites

Many of the following Websites need a Korean language program in order to run.

Ministry of Culture and Tourism
www.mct.go.kr

The National Museum of Korea
www.museum.go.kr

The National Museum of Contemporary Arts
www.moca.go.kr

The Korean Culture and Arts Foundation
www.kcaf.or.kr

The Korea National Tourism Organization
www.knto.or.kr

The Korea Sports Council
www.sports.or.kr

The Korea Institute for Youth Development
www.youthnet.re.kr

The Seoul Arts Center
www.sac.or.kr

The Korea Sport Science Institute
www.sports.re.kr

Chongdong Theater
www.chongdong.com

Korean National University of the Arts
www.knua.ac.kr

The National Council of Sports
www.sports-net.or.kr

About the Author

L. Robert Kohls is a Koreanist and one of the founders of the intercultural field. It was with the Peace Corps that he had his start as a cross-cultural trainer in the mid-1960s. His life-long love affair with Korea began in 1945, near the end of World War II, when he had the opportunity to get to know Korea as part of the U.S. troops who liberated Korea from the Japanese Colonial Empire. He is currently professor of East Asian Studies at the Center for the Pacific Rim at the University of San Francisco.

As a cross-cultural trainer, he has focused on preparing Americans to live and work not only in Korea but in all of Asia. His clients have been U.S. businesspeople and their spouses (from more than 70 of the Fortune 500 companies), diplomats (for ten years as a Foreign Service officer, he was given full charge of preparing the cultural attachés and press attachés serving at U.S. embassies around the world), Fulbright scholars, teachers, students, military personnel, Peace Corps volunteers, missionaries, and foreign nationals (from 150 countries) who study or work in the United States. He is also well known as a trainer of other cross-cultural trainers (in the most recent course, the trainees he taught had 440 years of collective overseas living experience). His

book *Survival Kit for Overseas Living,* in its fourth edition,
remains the best-selling Intercultural Press book.

Kohls has worked and done research in more than ninety
countries, and he and his wife have lived not only in Asia
(China and Japan as well as Korea) but also in Europe, Latin
America, the Middle East, and Africa.